THE SKILLS OF CAREER COUNSELING

THE SKILLS OF CAREER COUNSELING

PSYCHIATRIC REHABILITATION PRACTICE SERIES:book 4

Richard M. Pierce, Ph.D.
Director of Training Services
Carkhuff Institute of Human Technology
Amherst, Massachusetts

Mikal R. Cohen, Ph.D.
Director of Training, Center for Rehabilitation
   Research and Training in Mental Health
Research Associate Professor
Department of Rehabilitation Counseling
Sargent College of Allied Health Professions
Boston University

William A. Anthony, Ph.D.
Director, Center for Rehabilitation Research and
   Training in Mental Health
Associate Professor
Department of Rehabilitation Counseling
Sargent College of Allied Health Professions
Boston University

Barry F. Cohen, Ph.D.
Director of Health Care Services
Carkhuff Institute of Human Technology
Amherst, Massachusetts

Theodore W. Friel, Ph.D.
Director of Management Systems
Carkhuff Institute of Human Technology
Amherst, Massachusetts

University Park Press
Baltimore

UNIVERSITY PARK PRESS
International Publishers in Science, Medicine, and Education
233 East Redwood Street
Baltimore, Maryland 21202

This book was developed by the Carkhuff Institute of Human Technology, 22 Amherst Road, Amherst, MA 01002, pursuant to Public Health Service Grant No. T21 MH 14502-20 with the National Institute of Mental Health; Alcohol, Drug Abuse, and Mental Health Administration, Department of Health, Education and Welfare.

THE PSYCHIATRIC REHABILITATION PRACTICE SERIES

Instructor's Guide
by *William A. Anthony, Ph.D.,*
Mikal R. Cohen, Ph.D., and Richard M. Pierce, Ph.D.

Book 1: **The Skills of Diagnostic Planning** / *William A. Anthony, Richard M. Pierce, Mikal R. Cohen, and John R. Cannon*

Book 2: **The Skills of Rehabilitation Programming** / *William A. Anthony, Richard M. Pierce, Mikal R. Cohen, and John R. Cannon*

Book 3: **The Skills of Professional Evaluation** / *Mikal R. Cohen, William A. Anthony, Richard M. Pierce, Leroy A. Spaniol, and John R. Cannon*

Book 4: **The Skills of Career Counseling** / *Richard M. Pierce, Mikal R. Cohen, William A. Anthony, Barry F. Cohen, and Theodore W. Friel*

Book 5: **The Skills of Career Placement** / *Richard M. Pierce, Mikal R. Cohen, William A. Anthony, Barry F. Cohen, and Theodore W. Friel*

Book 6: **The Skills of Community Service Coordination** / *Mikal R. Cohen, Raphael L. Vitalo, William A. Anthony, and Richard M. Pierce*

Library of Congress Cataloging in Publication Data
Main entry under title:

The skills of career counseling.
  (Psychiatric rehabilitation practice series; book 4)
  Bibliography: p.
  1. Mentally ill—Rehabilitation. 2. Vocational guidance. 3. Vocational rehabilitation. I. Pierce, Richard M. II. Series.
[RC439.5.S53]   362.2'04256   79-29688
ISBN 0-8391-1579-2

THE SKILLS OF CAREER COUNSELING

CONTENTS

ABOUT THE AUTHORS

Dr. William A. Anthony is an Associate Professor and Director of Clinical Training in the Department of Rehabilitation Counseling, Sargent College of Allied Health Professions, Boston University. Dr. Anthony has been Project Director of a National Institute of Mental Health grant designed to develop and evaluate training materials for persons studying and practicing in the field of Psychiatric Rehabilitation. Dr. Anthony has been involved in the field of Psychiatric Rehabilitation in several different capacities. He has researched various aspects of psychiatric rehabilitation practice and has authored over three dozen articles about psychiatric rehabilitation which have appeared in professional journals.

Dr. Richard M. Pierce is Director of Training Services at the Carkhuff Institute of Human Technology, a non-profit organization dedicated to increasing human effectiveness. Dr. Pierce has extensive counseling experience and has consulted to dozens of local, state and federal human service programs. He has taught the skills and knowledge of psychiatric rehabilitation to practitioners from a variety of disciplines. Dr. Pierce is noted for his research on the training of counselors. Dr. Pierce has authored eight books and dozens of articles in professional journals.

Dr. Mikal R. Cohen is the Director of Rehabilitation and Mental Health Services at the Carkhuff Institute of Human Technology, a non-profit organization dedicated to increasing human effectiveness. Dr. Cohen has been a practitioner in several outpatient and inpatient mental health settings, and has served as an administrator, inservice trainer, program evaluator and consultant to numerous rehabilitation and mental health programs. She has developed teaching curricula and taught the skills of psychiatric rehabilitation to practitioners throughout the United States. Furthermore, Dr. Cohen has authored a number of books and articles in the fields of mental health and health care.

Dr. Barry F. Cohen is Director of Health Services Programs at the Carkhuff Institute of Human Technology. Dr. Cohen has had extensive experience in several mental health settings as an administrator, staff trainer and consultant. He has been the administrator of a community mental health center and has led faculty development workshops for health care faculty throughout the United States. Dr. Cohen has authored numerous publications in the fields of mental health and health care services.

Dr. Theodore W. Friel is Director of Management Systems at the Carkhuff Institute of Human Technology. Formerly with IBM, Dr. Friel is best known for his award-winning development of the Educational and Career Exploration System (ECES), a computer-based career guidance program which, in 1974, was hailed as "the program of the 1980's". He is currently developing management and training systems designed to increase the effectiveness of human service organizations. Dr. Friel is the author of eight books and numerous professional articles.

CARKHUFF INSTITUTE of HUMAN TECHNOLOGY

The Carkhuff Institute of Human Technology is intended to serve as a non-profit international center for the creation, development and application of human technology. The Institute, the first of its kind anywhere in the world, takes its impetus from the comprehensive human resource development models of Dr. Robert R. Carkhuff. Using these models as functional prototypes, the Institute's people synthesize human experience and objective technology in the form of a wide range of specific programs and applications.

We live in a complex technological society. Only recently have we begun to recognize and struggle with two crucially important facts: improperly used, our technology creates as many problems as it solves; and this same technology has been delivered to us with no apparent control or "off" buttons. Our attempts to retreat to some pretechnological, purely humanistic state have been both foolish and ill-fated. If we are to develop our resources and actualize our real potential, we must learn to grow in ways which integrate our scientific and applied knowledge about the human condition with the enduring human values which alone can make our growth meaningful.

We cannot afford to waste more time in fragmentary and ill-conceived endeavors. The next several decades — and perhaps far less than that — will be a critical period in our collective history. Recognizing this, the Carkhuff Institute of Human Technology is dedicated to fostering the growth and development of personnel who can develop, plan, implement and evaluate human resource development programs while making direct contributions to the scientific and technological bases of these same programs. Thus the Institute's fundamental mission is to integrate full technical potency with fully human and humane goals — in other words, to deliver skills to people which let them become effective movers and creators rather than impotent victims.

CARKHUFF INSTITUTE of HUMAN TECHNOLOGY

22 AMHERST ROAD
AMHERST, MA 01002
(413) 256-0169

PSYCHIATRIC REHABILITATION PRACTICE SERIES

PREFACE

This text is one of a series of six books designed to facilitate the teaching of various psychiatric rehabilitation skills. It is written for professionals practicing in the field as well as for students studying in such professions as nursing, rehabilitation counseling, occupational therapy, psychology, psychiatry, and social work. Each of these disciplines has contributed and will continue to contribute practitioners, researchers, administrators, and teachers to the field of psychiatric rehabilitation.

This series of training manuals evolved from a lengthy analysis of the practitioner skills that seemed to facilitate the rehabilitation outcome of persons with psychiatric disabilities. Under the sponsorship of the National Institute of Mental Health, each of these training manuals was developed and then field-tested on a group of rehabilitation mental health professionals and students. Based on the feedback of the training participants after the use of these skills with psychiatrically disabled clients, each training manual was revised. Thus, the content of the books reflects not only the authors' perspectives, but also the ideas of the initial group of training participants.

The ultimate purpose of this six-volume series is to improve the rehabilitation services that are presently offered to the psychiatrically disabled person. This training text is written for those practitioners whose rehabilitation mission is either: (1) to assist in the reintegration of the psychiatrically disabled client into the community; or (2) to maintain the ability of the formerly disabled client to continue functioning in the community and, in so doing, to prevent a reoccurrence of psychiatric disability. In other words, depending upon a client's particular situation, psychiatric rehabilitation practitioners attempt either to reduce their clients' dependence on the mental health system or maintain whatever level of independence the clients have already been able to achieve.

This mission can be accomplished when the focus of the psychiatric rehabilitation practitioner's concern is increasing the *skills* and *abilities* of the psychiatrically disabled client. More specifically, the rehabilitation practitioner works to promote the client's ability to employ those skills necessary to live, learn, and/or work in the community. Success is achieved when the client is able to function in the community as independently as possible.

Historically, the primary focus in psychiatric rehabilitation has been on the development of alternative living, learning, and working environments. In such environments, psychiatrically disabled clients have been provided settings in which they can function at a reduced level of skilled performance that is still higher than the level of functioning typically demanded in an institutional setting. In addition, these rehabilitation settings have provided a more humane, active, and "normal" environment within which clients can function. The hope has been that, over a period of time, the more positive environment of these rehabilitation settings might help many clients to improve their ability to function more independently and, in many cases, to actually leave the rehabilitation setting.

Within the last decade, however, rehabilitation has come to involve much more than the development, administration, and coordination of specific settings. Psychiatric rehabilitation practitioners can now assume a direct rehabilitation role by *diagnosing critical skill deficits* in their clients and *prescribing rehabilitation programs* designed to overcome these skill deficits. The development of rehabilitation settings that emphasize the skills and abilities of the clients has helped lay the foundation for this approach to psychiatric rehabilitation.

Although the greatest boon to rehabilitation within the mental health system has been the development of new and unique environmental settings as alternatives to institutional living, the most significant failure of psychiatric rehabilitation has been its inability to train the psychiatric rehabilitation practitioner thoroughly in rehabilitation skills. Professionals from a wide range of disciplines (e.g., counseling, nursing, psychiatry, social work, and psychology) engage in the practice of psychiatric rehabilitation. For the most part, however, these various disciplines have only the expertise developed in their own professions to bring to the field of psychiatric rehabilitation. Their training has lacked a specific set of rehabilitation skills to complement the expertise of their own disciplines.

The present series of psychiatric rehabilitation training texts, of which this volume is a part, is designed to help overcome the lack of specialized training in psychiatric rehabilitation. These training books focus on the specific skills areas that are designed to equip the psychiatric rehabilitation practitioner with the expertise necessary to promote the abilities of the psychiatrically disabled client, either by increasing the client's skills and by modifying the environment so as to better accommodate the client's present level of skilled behavior.

The first two training books help the psychiatric rehabilitation practitioner to become more proficient in *diagnosing* and *teaching* the skills that the client needs to function more effectively in the community. The third book provides the practitioner with the skills necessary to *evaluate* the outcome of her or his rehabilitative efforts. Training books four and five focus specifically on practitioner skills that have been the traditional concern of the rehabilitation practitioner — *career counseling* and *career placement* skills. The sixth training book focuses on ways in which the rehabilitation practitioner can *use the resources of the community* to better accommodate the client's present abilities and programming needs.

Although each text is part of a series of training books, each has been designed so that it may be used independently of the other. The six books included in the series are:

1. **The Skills of Diagnostic Planning**
2. **The Skills of Rehabilitation Programming**
3. **The Skills of Professional Evaluation**
4. **The Skills of Career Counseling**
5. **The Skills of Career Placement**
6. **The Skills of Community Service Coordination**

The skills-learning *process* within the training books involves an explain-demonstrate-practice format. That is, the practitioner is first explained the skill, is then shown examples of the skill, and finally is provided with suggestions on how to practice or do the skill. The practice suggestions include first practicing in a simulated situation and then actually performing the skill with a psychiatrically disabled client.

The first chapter of each training book overviews the specific practitioner skills that comprise that text. The next several chapters of each text are the teaching chapters and present the explain-demonstrate-practice steps involved in learning each specific skill. The final chapter of each book suggests ways in which the practitioner can evaluate one's own or another person's performance of these skills. The reference section of the books contains the major references that are sources of further discussion of various aspects of the skills.

Each of the major teaching chapters has a vignette at the beginning and end of the chapter. This vignette or short story is designed to illustrate unsuccessful and successful applications of the specific skills that are the focus of that particular chapter. Its purpose is to give the reader an overview of the skills that are presented in each chapter. In addition, a summary of the skill behaviors that comprise each major skill is given at the end of each chapter section.

Each chapter contains practice suggestions for each skill that can facilitate the learners' practice of their newly developing skills. Often the learner is first asked to practice and demonstrate her or his skill learning by filling out some type of table or chart. These charts can serve as an observable demonstration of the learner's mastery of a particular skill. Most of these various charts are not needed in the day-to-day application of these skills with actual clients. However, during the skill-learning process, these charts or tables are useful in demonstrating the learner's present level of skill mastery, either to the learner her or himself or to the learner's supervisors and teachers.

The skill-learning *outcome* of each of these training volumes is an observable, measurable cluster of practitioner skills. These skills are not meant to replace the skills of the various disciplines currently involved in the practice of psychiatric rehabilitation; rather, these skills are seen as complementary to the professional's existing skills. The additional use of these rehabilitation skills can play an extremely important role in improving the efficacy of psychiatric rehabilitation.

The Psychiatric Rehabilitation Practice Series has developed out of the contributions of a number of different people. We are particularly indebted to a great many students and practicing professionals, who, by virtue of their willingness to learn these skills and provide knowledge as to their effectiveness, have allowed us the opportunity to develop, refine, and revise these texts.

We would also like to acknowledge the individual instructors who taught the first group of students from these texts, and gave willingly of their time and talents in the development of this series.

These initial instructors were Arthur Dell Orto, Marianne Farkas, Robert Lasky, Patrice Muchowske, Paul Power, Don Shrey and LeRoy Spaniol.

Particular appreciation is expressed to Marianne Farkas, who not only taught these skills, but who also assisted in the editing and evaluation of these training texts.

Boston, Massachusetts

W.A.A.

M.R.C.

R.M.P.

THE SKILLS OF CAREER COUNSELING

Chapter 1 *THE CAREER COUNSELING MODEL*

Stated most broadly, the goal of psychiatric rehabilitation is to restore to clients their capacity to function in the community. Philosophically, this means that rehabilitation is directed at increasing the *strengths* of the clients so that they can achieve their maximum potential for independent living and meaningful careers. Although many traditional treatment approaches seek to prepare clients to function independently, the emphasis in traditional psychiatric treatment has typically been on the reduction of client discomfort by changing underlying personality structures, increasing client insights, and alleviating symptomatology.

Although the total treatment process for disabled psychiatric clients includes aspects of both traditional psychiatric treatment and psychiatric therapy and rehabilitation, it is important that these activities be separated conceptually so that the rehabilitation process receives the emphasis necessary to develop its own unique contribution to client care.

This text represents one of a series of books whose purpose is to define and teach the unique skills of psychiatric rehabilitation. The particular skill with which this book is concerned is that of *career counseling*.

THE DEFINITION, PURPOSE, AND APPLICATIONS OF CAREER COUNSELING

WHAT CAREER COUNSELING IS

The word "career" is derived from the French word "carrière," meaning a high road or racecourse. *Webster's New World Dictionary* defines *career* as follows:

> l. originally a racing course; hence 2. a swift course as of the sun through the sky; hence 3. full speed, 4. one's progress through life, 5. one's advancement or achievement in a particular occupation; hence 6. a life work; profession; occupation.

For the purposes of this book, "career development" refers to the process by which the psychiatrically disabled client can efficiently and effectively develop and pursue occupational goals. Career counseling, then, refers to those skilled activities of the rehabilitation practitioner that facilitate the client's career development.

WHY CAREER COUNSELING IS IMPORTANT

The purpose of career counseling is to equip the client with the skills and knowledge needed to choose a career goal and develop a career plan. There are many ways of choosing or, more correctly, *not* choosing a career. Research reported by Friel suggests that less than a quarter of the population makes decisions by weighing the facts and planning carefully (Friel and Carkhuff, 1974). And even these few do not approach the decision-making and planning process in any systematic fashion.

Many psychiatrically disabled clients acquiesce to the wishes of others. If their friends, family, or other relatives find them a job, they will invariably take it. If the rehabilitation or other mental health practitioner recommends an occupation, they will pursue it. Such clients have difficulty making decisions and, once they have made one, accepting responsibility for the decision. It is not they who succeed or fail but the advice that has been given them. And because it is frequently the case that the advice is not derived from a comprehensive understanding of the client, the risk of failure is great.

Other clients act impetuously. They do not explore or try to understand either themselves or the world of work. They simply act. The consequences of such unplanned actions are often quite negative.

There are many other ways in which clients make career decisions. Some are fatalistically resigned to whatever happens, others rely on intuition, and the remainder just agonize or are paralyzed in the face of the decision.

Anthony has summarized data that indicate that only 25 percent of ex-psychiatric patients are able to remain competitively employed, regardless of the follow-up period studied (Anthony, 1979). Other research has shown that obtaining and maintaining employment is a key factor in the attainment of rehabilitation goals (Pierce, 1975). More specifically, it has been found that rehabilitative recidivism is reduced when the client is able to work. Collingwood found that simply having a clear-cut occupational goal was related to reduced recidivism (Collingwood, 1976).

In essence, the need for the practitioner to possess career counseling skills is based on two assumptions. First, most psychiatrically disabled clients do not know how to make carefully planned career decisions or how to develop effective career plans. Second, they need to learn to make more satisfying career decisions and more systematic career plans because their future is significantly related to their career choices and plans.

WHEN AND WHERE CAREER COUNSELING CAN BE USED

Career counseling is appropriate for any psychiatrically disabled client who is diagnosed as having one or more deficiencies in the career development area. In general, clients' career deficits often revolve around a lack of career information; they lack knowledge about their own work interests and values and/or about how the world of work is organized. In addition, clients may not know how to use the information they have about themselves and the world of work to make career decisions. Also, clients often do not know how to develop and implement the necessary steps capable of getting them to their career goals.

The following are examples of typical client deficits in the area of career development:

I. Inability to identify realistic job alternatives:

    A. The client lacks information about self.

        1. The client does not know what general interests and values to consider in choosing an occupation.
        2. The client does not know her or his abilities or deficits in relation to the world of work.

    B. The client lacks information about the world of work.

        1. The client does not know what occupations relate to his or her interests.
        2. The client does not know what occupations relate to his or her abilities or deficits.

II. Inability to decide upon a realistic and satisfying job goal:

    A. The client does not know how to specifically identify her or his most important career values.

    B. The client does not have the detailed occupational information to evaluate potential occupations.

    C. The client does not have a systematic method for making a career decision based on his or her values and occupational information.

III. Inability to develop a step-by-step plan capable of achieving the occupational goal:

    A. The client is unable to identify in concrete terms the deficits that are interfering with attainment of the occupational goal.

    B. The client is unable to identify in concrete, specific, and achievable terms the steps that can be taken to overcome these deficits.

Clearly, clients may not have deficiencies in all these areas, though they frequently do. Where there is a deficiency in only one or two areas, the practitioner obviously needs to use only those skills necessary to facilitate the client's career development in those specific career areas. For example, the client may only need to develop a step-by-step plan for reaching an occupational objective. Or the client may only want to evaluate a decision already reached. Although any particular client may not need to progress through all the steps in this book, the rehabilitation practitioner will want to master all the skills so that she/he can mix and match the skills to suit a particular client's career deficits.

The practitioner can facilitate the diagnosis of the specific career counseling needs of the client by using the evaluation checklist outlined in the last chapter of this book (Table 49). The practitioner can then use that part of the career counseling program that will best meet the client's diagnosed career needs. The client's career deficits and strengths may also be diagnosed during the more comprehensive diagnostic planning process (see Book 1 in this series), when the client's skill behaviors in living, learning, and working environments are assessed. Many of the diagnosed client deficits that affect the client's functioning in the working environment can then be treated by using either the career counseling skills of this book or the career placement skills outlined in Book 5 of this series.

Career counseling skills are seen as appropriate for anyone who is working or planning to work with psychiatrically disabled clients, whether inpatients or outpatients, in order to assist them in living and working more independently. Career counseling is seen as an appropriate activity at any point during the rehabilitation process. That is, it can occur prior to initiation of the rehabilitation process, concurrently with the process, or even after the process has been completed. Portions of the skills can also be used in controlled or sheltered environments with clients who are functioning at low levels. For example, the skills can be used to explore what type of sheltered workshop experience might be best for the client; or the client can begin to learn career decision-making skills by deciding which job to perform within a particular sheltered workshop. The determining criterion is the point at which it becomes functional for the client to begin planning his or her occupational life in a systematic way.

The practitioner can work with clients to develop their careers in individual or group settings. In general, a group context has several advantages. First, a group approach is more efficient in terms of the practitioner's time. Second, clients working in a group can exchange ideas about choosing an occupation, the available alternatives, and other similar concerns.

THE STAGES AND SKILLS OF CAREER COUNSELING

This book will focus in detail on how career counseling is accomplished. The purpose of this introduction is to overview the processes involved. Simply stated, the ultimate goal of career development is for the clients to develop career objectives and specific and effective plans for reaching those objectives.

In order to accomplish this goal, the clients proceed through three basic and developmental stages: (1) an *exploration* stage, (2) an *understanding* stage, and (3) an *action* stage. Each of these stages has an observable outcome.

Table 1. The Stages and Skills of Career Counseling

I. *Exploring the client's career alternatives*

    A. Exploring information about the client's world

    B. Exploring information about the world of work in relation to the client's world

II. *Understanding the client's career alternatives*

    A. Understanding the client's unique career value system

    B. Understanding the world of work in relation to the client's career value system

III. *Acting on the client's career choice*

    A. Acting to develop a career plan

    B. Acting to implement the career plan

In the initial *exploration* stage, the practitioner helps the clients explore both the world of work and themselves. In particular, the clients first explore the personal interests and values that they feel are important in selecting an occupation. They then explore the way the world of work is organized in terms of personal interest patterns. Finally, the clients explore the way the world of work is organized in terms of occupational requirements. The outcome of the exploration stage is the identification of a number of realistic job alternatives.

The exploration stage eventually gives way to the *understanding* stage. During this stage, the practitioner seeks to help the clients understand exactly what their personal values mean. The practitioner then works with the clients to evaluate various occupational alternatives in terms of these values. The outcome of the understanding stage is the selection by the clients of realistic and satisfying occupational goals.

Finally, the clients are ready for the *action* stage of career development. During this stage, the practitioner first works with the clients to develop specific plans that will lead to achievement of the occupational objectives developed in the second stage. Second, the practitioner works with the clients to develop implementation schedules. By developing career plans and implementation schedules with the clients, the practitioner has helped teach them how to make future modifications in their career plans if necessary. An ability to modify the career plan is necessary for a variety of reasons (e.g., new opportunities open up, new things are learned). It is important that the clients learn to modify their career routes in order to continue along the path to their career objectives and/or to modify those objectives. The outcome of the action stage is the client's possession of a step-by-step plan of action to achieve specific career goals. The stages and skills of effective career counseling are presented in Table 1. Table 2 outlines each skill.

Table 2. Outline of the Skills of Career Counseling

I. *Exploring information about the client's world*
    A. Exploring previous educational and work experiences
    B. Exploring general interests
    C. Exploring career values

II. *Exploring information about the world of work in relation to the client's world*
    A. Exploring work/interest areas
    B. Identifying preferred work/interest area
    C. Exploring educational requirement categories
    D. Identifying preferred educational requirement category
    E. Expanding the number of realistic occupational alternatives

III. *Understanding the client's unique career value system*
    A. Defining career values
    B. Scaling career values
    C. Weighing career values

IV. *Understanding the world of work in relation to the client's career value system*
    A. Investigating specific occupational alternatives
    B. Making career decisions using values/occupational knowledge
    C. Developing new understanding through an internship experience

V. *Acting to develop a career plan*
    A. Identifying and categorizing problems
    B. Assessing present problem behavior
    C. Assessing the needed goal level
    D. Developing career steps to the needed goals

VI. *Acting to implement the career plan*
    A. Specifying needed resources
    B. Assigning completion dates

In order to guide a client through the three stages of career development, the practitioner needs two sets of skills. The first set consists of the career counseling skills themselves. That is, the practitioner needs to master the content of career development. This is, of course, the focus of this book.

Second, the practitioner needs structured interviewing skills. These skills have been discussed in detail in Book 1 of this series, and that discussion will not be repeated here. Suffice it to say at this point that the practitioner needs a minimum of three structured interviewing skills — responding to content, responding to feeling, and responding to feeling and content.

Responding to content involves the ability to accurately summarize the client's verbal expressions. A format that can be used is "You're saying _____" or "In other words, _____." Below is an example:

Client statement: Gee, I really don't know what kind of job I want. I've really tried, but I just can't think of anything that really sounds good.

Practitioner response to content: You're saying that no jobs you've been able to think of sound especially appealing.

In a response to feeling, the practitioner responds to the client's feelings about the content. A format to use is "You feel _____." Thus, the practitioner might respond to the above as follows:

Practitioner response to feeling: You feel discouraged.

At the third level of response, the practitioner responds to both feeling and content at the same time. The format here is "You _____ because _____." To the earlier client statement, the practitioner might say:

Practitioner response to feeling and content: You feel discouraged because no jobs you've been able to think of sound especially appealing.

These types of responses are important for several reasons. First, they enable the practitioner to ascertain whether she or he really understands the situation. Second, by showing understanding, the responses encourage the client to discuss the problem further; a number of research studies (Cannon and Pierce, 1968; Truax and Carkhuff, 1967) have reported a causal relationship between client self-exploration and practitioner response. Third, research evidence also supports a positive correlation between these interpersonal skills and various measures of client vocational rehabilitation outcome (Bozarth and Rubin, 1975). Whether the practitioner responds to content, feeling, or both will depend on whether she or he wants the client to talk more about the content, the feeling, or both.

In summary, then, the practitioner will need both the structured interviewing skills cited above and an expertise in those specific skills necessary to guide the client effectively through the stages of career development. The intent of this book is to increase the practitioner's career counseling skills. In addition to these skills, however, the practitioner needs knowledge of the current issues in vocational assessments and vocational theory (e.g., see Isaacson, 1977; Holland, 1973; Hoppock, 1976; Pruitt, 1977).

In learning the many skills of career counseling, the practitioner may feel overwhelmed by the amount of time involved in guiding a client through all the career counseling steps. There is no doubt that skillful career counseling consumes more time than simply trying to place a client in an available slot. Large caseloads, little direct service time, and numerous recording forms all seem to work against the possibility of a comprehensive career counseling process. As mentioned previously, not all clients require the use of all these skill steps. However, many psychiatrically disabled clients do, in fact, need to be counseled more skillfully and comprehensively. The high recidivism and unemployment rates of psychiatrically disabled clients clearly indicate this need. The practitioner beginning to master the skills of career counseling, therefore, may wish to consider restructuring his or her time to allow for greater use of these skills. If the amount of time available for career counseling is limited, a practitioner skilled in the entire spectrum of career counseling will be in a better position to make the most appropriate modifications and take the most helpful shortcuts. Many clients will be able to work independently on the career counseling steps; this will, of course, depend on such client skills as the ability to follow written and verbal directions and the ability to record information.

Some practitioners may typically refer their clients to other agencies for career counseling. By learning the skills outlined in this book, these practitioners will be able to make a more detailed and comprehensive referral; the practitioner can inform the agencies of what is expected of them and thus hold these agencies accountable for achieving specific career outcomes.

Chapter 2 EXPLORING THE CLIENT'S CAREER ALTERNATIVES ▰

EXPLORING CAREER ALTERNATIVES: AN UNSKILLED APPROACH

Ken looked down at the open file on his desk, then up at the woman who sat across from him. "Well, Jocelyn, the main thing we've got to do is see about finding you a job."

Jocelyn nodded. "Yeah, I guess."

"Why don't you tell me a little about your background? You said you finished high school, right?"

"Uh-huh. John Jay High, over on the other side of town. I mean, I never did really great there or anything, but I got through. I guess that's all that really counts."

Ken nodded in a noncommital fashion. "What sorts of courses did you take there that you might be able to put to use on the job?"

"Courses?" Jocelyn grimaced and shrugged. "I don't know whether I ever learned anything there that I could really use. It was all really dull stuff, really a drag."

"Well ... Did you ever take any courses related to any kind of office work?"

"Yeah, I guess so. I took a couple of semesters of typing. And I took this dumb course in office procedures or something like that."

"Did you do OK in them?" Ken asked, making a note on his pad.

Jocelyn shrugged again. "I guess so. Like I said, I passed. And I can still type OK. My sister's got this old typewriter, only she doesn't know how to use it. I promised her I'd teach her how."

Ken smiled, pleased to find that Jocelyn's situation could be handled so easily. "That's great, Jocelyn," he said. "Listen, as long as you can type and handle the most basic kinds of office work, there's no reason you can't find a job right away."

"Yeah?"

Ken nodded. "Sure! Secretaries are always in demand." He wrote out some information on a card and handed it to Jocelyn. "Look. Here's the name of a good employment agency. I've referred a number of clients to them. You just go on down there and tell them you're looking for secretarial work. I bet they've got something just right for you!"

By now Ken was standing. Jocelyn rose, looking from the card to Ken and back to the card. "You think it'll be pretty simple, huh?" Her voice sounded somewhat skeptical.

"Absolutely! Take it from me, you'll be working by the end of this week."

And Ken was absolutely right. By week's end, Jocelyn was on the payroll at Brooks Stationery Co., doing light typing and answering the phone. Everything was settled — or so at least it seemed until two weeks later when Ken got a call from his friend at the employment agency.

"Listen, that last client of yours — Jocelyn? She walked out on Brooks last Friday."

"Really?" Although similar things had happened before, Ken was still surprised. "Did she tell them why?"

"Uh-huh. According to her, she just didn't like working in an office."

In order to act effectively, clients need to know about themselves and the world of work. If clients are deficient in these areas, they need to first *explore themselves* and then *explore the world of work*. The specific client career deficits that are addressed by this chapter include: (1) lack of comprehensive knowledge about what general interests and values are important in choosing an occupation; (2) lack of knowledge about personal abilities in relation to the world of work; (3) lack of knowledge about what occupations are related to personal interests; and (4) lack of knowledge about what occupations are related to personal abilities. The result of any or all of these client deficits is the client's inability to identify several realistic alternatives.

Although the above are common deficits that any client may have, they will usually not be stated in the above manner by either a referral agency or the client. Common problems that could indicate deficits in the above areas are:

1. The client needs or wants to know about a particular job.
2. The client has no idea what she or he is suited for.
3. The client has so many options she or he does not know where to start.
4. The client's job expectations seem unrealistic.

In essence, *these exploration skills are appropriate whenever a client does not have several specific and realistic alternative occupations from which to choose.* The kinds of statements initially made by the client are frequently too vague for the rehabilitation practitioner to know for sure what specific deficits may be involved, and the practitioner will have to obtain enough additional input from the client. For example, the practitioner might ask whether the client knows of any occupations in which she or he might be interested. If the answer is "I don't know any," or if the client can name only two or three alternatives, a lack of knowledge about occupations related to interests is indicated. The practitioner might then follow up by exploring the specific factors the client wishes to consider in choosing an occupation. Again, if the client's answer is "I don't know," or if the client can identify only two or three criteria, a deficit is indicated in knowledge about what is important to the client in choosing an occupation. (Before any career counseling steps are implemented, the client must accept the idea that he or she actually has deficits in the career development area. The practitioner interviewing and assessment skills that facilitate the client "owning" his or her strengths and deficits are presented in Book 1 of this series, *The Skills of Diagnostic Planning.*)

The remainder of this chapter will address the specific career counseling skills needed to overcome the general knowledge deficits about self and work — the skills, that is, that are needed to generate some initial occupational alternatives. These skills are summarized in Table 3.

Table 3.   Outline of the Skills of Exploring Career Alternatives

I.   Exploring information about the client's world

    A.   Exploring previous educational and work experiences
    B.   Exploring general interests
    C.   Exploring career values

II.   Exploring information about the world of work in relation to the client's world

    A.   Exploring work/interest areas
    B.   Identifying preferred work/interest area
    C.   Exploring educational requirement categories
    D.   Identifying preferred educational requirement category
    E.   Expanding the number of realistic occupational alternatives

EXPLORING INFORMATION ABOUT THE CLIENT'S WORLD

Many psychiatrically disabled clients are reluctant to explore their worlds. They do not experience a level of self-worth that would allow them to feel that self-exploration would have a beneficial effect on their problems. For this reason, they often tend to accept suggestions passively. It is as if they are saying, "I am not worth discussing." In order to be most effective in the process of career counseling, however, the practitioner will want to engage clients in the process of self-exploration.

By helping clients to explore general feelings or thoughts about themselves in relation to career choices, the practitioner can establish a basis of trust on which to begin gathering information that the clients may be sensitive about or reluctant to disclose.

11

EXPLORING EDUCATIONAL EXPERIENCE

The first step in obtaining information is to explore with the client his or her educational background in relation to careers. The main purpose here is for the practitioner to learn about the client's educational history in relation to the world of work. The process involves a structured interview. In particular, educational information should be gathered relative to (1) school name, (2) dates attended, (3) certificates received, (4) area of study, (5) areas of interest, and (6) areas of competence. A form in which this information can be summarized is portrayed in Table 4.

Gathering information about school name, dates attended, and certificates received requires no further explanation. "Area of study" refers to the client's area of major educational emphasis. For example, at a high school level the major area might be auto mechanics or college preparation; at the college level, the major might be history or engineering. Information should also be obtained about other areas in which a client took a number of courses (i.e., areas of minor emphasis). If the practitioner is uncertain as to what a particular area of study entailed, she or he will want to find out what courses were taken by the client that relate to the major. The goal is to understand the client's educational preparation.

In the area of the client's interests, the practitioner will want to know the areas of study and/or specific courses the client particularly liked and the reasons why. Understanding the reason for liking a course will help the practitioner to know whether the client was interested in the material itself or whether the interest was only situationally specific (perhaps related to a particular teacher or study activity used in the course). Finally, the practitioner can gather a fuller picture of the client's interests by exploring those areas of study and/or specific courses that the client particularly disliked. Again, it is critical to understand the reason for the dislike in order to tie the feeling to the content or to something about the specific situation.

Exploration of "competence" means defining the areas or specific courses in which the client performed either particularly well or poorly. Such exploration can be handled in terms of grades as well as by discussion of the client's subjective impressions of where she or he experienced difficulty or performed with ease. As with the interest area, it is important here to explore with the client the reasons for success or failure so that the practitioner can obtain an accurate perspective.

In conducting this type of structured interview, it is best to begin with the client's most recent educational experience and work backward. The most recent experience is the one the client can best recall; beginning here will build success into the interview for the client. In addition, because the most recent educational experience is frequently the most advanced, it is often the most important and the most relevant. If the practitioner understands this experience, it may not be necessary to

Table 4. Summary Form for Client Educational Experiences

Educational Experience Summary

School
Name: _____ Dates Attended: _____ to _____ Certificate: _____

Major Area
of Study: _____

Minor Area
of Study: _____

Related Course Titles	Related Course Titles
1. _____	1. _____
2. _____	2. _____
3. _____	3. _____
4. _____	4. _____
5. _____	5. _____
6. _____	6. _____
7. _____	7. _____
8. _____	8. _____
9. _____	9. _____
10. _____	10. _____

Areas or Courses Particularly Liked	Areas or Courses Particularly Disliked
Title *Reason*	*Title* *Reason*
1. _____	1. _____
2. _____	2. _____
3. _____	3. _____
4. _____	4. _____

Areas of Particular Competence	Areas of Particular Difficulty
Asset *Reason*	*Deficit* *Reason*
1. _____	1. _____
2. _____	2. _____
3. _____	3. _____
4. _____	4. _____

explore previous educational experiences. For example, if a client has completed high school, there will usually be little need to explore the junior high experience. On the other hand, if a client's most recent educational experience has been incomplete, relatively brief, disliked, or a failure, it may well be necessary to look at a previous educational experience. For example, if the client has taken only one or two courses at a community college, it will be necessary to go back and look at the high school experience in order to really understand the client's educational background. By the same token, if a client's most recent experience was the GED, it would be appropriate to look at the high school or junior high record to understand the other courses to which the client had been exposed and which might have vocational implications. A third example might involve a college graduate who did poorly in many courses and/or was very unhappy with them. In this case, the high school experience might reveal other areas of interest and/or competence.

The practitioner will also want to overview the structured interview with the client. In other words, the practitioner can inform the client about the six areas they will be exploring. Ideally, the areas should be given to the client in writing. This will serve two purposes. First, it will enable the client to know where the process is going and thus to feel more comfortable with it. Second, the client may refer to a written overview in order to summarize new educational experiences. Thus, the practitioner may give the client a written form similar to the one illustrated in Table 4. The practitioner can also use a form such as this to record his or her own information about the client.

Information of this type may be developed by some clients independently of the practitioner. Some of this more factual information is often obtained on routine agency intake forms. However, there is value in engaging the client in an interview structured around these questions. Particularly important is client exploration around the issues of what courses were liked, disliked, and why; equally important is client exploration with respect to the course areas in which she/he feels most competent, least competent, and why. Client exploration stimulated by those issues may give the practitioner and client insights about client strengths and deficits of which they were previously unaware. Also, the focus on "reasons" will often guide the clients toward an exploration of their *feelings* about their careers. The counselor's ability to understand the clients' feelings about career-related content can encourage clients to become more deeply involved in their explorations of career issues.

Table 5 presents an example of a completed educational experience summary form. Harry is a young man who is currently out of work. This situation, along with other pressures in his home, has precipitated an emotional breakdown. He has expressed a wish to "find a more satisfactory job."

14

Table 5. Completed Summary Form for Client Educational Experiences

Educational Experience Summary

School Name: Monroe Tech. & Voc. H.S. Dates Attended: 1968 to 1972 Certificate: H.S. diploma

Major Area of Study: Auto Mechanics

Minor Area of Study: None

Related Course Titles	Related Course Titles
1. Auto Repair Shop I-IV	1.
2. Business Math I, II	2.
3.	3.
4.	4.
5.	5.
6.	6.
7.	7.
8.	8.
9.	9.
10.	10.

Areas or Courses Particularly Liked		Areas or Courses Particularly Disliked	
Title	*Reason*	*Title*	*Reason*
1. Auto Repair Lab	Like working with hands and actually fixing something	1. History	All memorizing
2.		2.	
3.		3.	
4.		4.	
5.		5.	

Areas of Particular Competence		Areas of Particular Difficulty	
Asset	*Reason*	*Deficit*	*Reason*
1. Got an A in all repair classes	Just comes easy	1. English	Words and grammar come hard
2.		2.	
3.		3.	
4.		4.	
5.		5.	

15

Practice Situations

Use a form similar to Table 4 to practice filling out an educational experience summary form for yourself. If you are currently in school, your most recent educational experience would be the one in which you are now enrolled. Once you have completed the practice exercise using yourself as the client, use a real client or a friend to practice obtaining a picture of his or her educational experience. Before you begin the process, remember to overview what you are going to do. Attempt to maximixe the person's involvement in the process by responding to the content and/or feelings that are presented by the individual in response to your questions.

EXPLORING WORK EXPERIENCE

The second major area that the practitioner needs to explore with the client is the client's work experience. The information obtained during this portion of the exploratory phase parallels the information obtained during the exploration of the client's educational experience. The purpose here is for the practitioner to emerge with an understanding of the client's previous job experience. In particular, the practitioner will need to gather data relative to (1) job titles, (2) employers, (3) dates of employment, (4) job duties and responsibilities, (5) areas of interest, and (6) areas of competence. A summary form for this information is shown in Table 6.

"Job Title" simple refers to the name of the job the client held. "Employer" refers to the company or agency that employed the client. It should be noted that the client may have held the same job with more than one employer. Similarly, the client may have held more than one job with the same employer. "Dates of Employment" refers to the dates the client held each job with each employer. "Major Duties and Responsibilities" is intended to provide a summary of the major activities that the client performed on the job. If the practitioner does not understand what a particular job activity involved, the client should be asked what had to be done to perform that duty. "Special Areas of Interest" addresses the specific activities and working conditions that the client particularly liked or disliked. Finally, "Special Areas of Competence" focuses on those activities in which the client felt particularly adept or inept. This exploration should focus not only on the client's effectiveness in using job skills *per se* but also on the client's dependability (e.g., attendance and punctuality) and ability to get along with other people.

As indicated in the earlier section on education, the practitioner can obtain a broader perspective on the information being presented by the client by exploring the reasons for the client's likes, dislikes, aptitudes, and deficiencies. In addition, the practitioner will find it very effective to adhere to the two principles of the structured career interview

Table 6. Summary Form for Client Work Experiences

Work Experience Summary

Job Title: _____

Employer Name		Dates of Employment
1. _____		_____ to _____
2. _____		_____ to _____
3. _____		_____ to _____

Major Duties and Responsibilities

1. _____
2. _____
3. _____
4. _____
5. _____

Special Areas of Interest

Liked	Reason	Disliked	Reason
1. _____		1. _____	
2. _____		2. _____	
3. _____		3. _____	
4. _____		4. _____	
5. _____		5. _____	

Special Areas of Competence

Asset	Reason	Deficit	Reason
1. _____		1. _____	
2. _____		2. _____	
3. _____		3. _____	
4. _____		4. _____	
5. _____		5. _____	

17

discussed earlier: (1) begin with the most recent work experience and move back to earlier experiences, and (2) overview with the client, preferably in writing, the areas that will be addressed. In fact, if the client's recent experiences are dominated by work rather than education, and/or if there is reason to believe that the client has been more successful at work than at school, then it is appropriate to explore the client's work experience before exploring the educational experience.

A sample format on which to record information concerning a client's work experience was presented in Table 6. There can be one such form for each job that is explored with the client. In most cases, the last five years is a sufficient period to explore (of course, if the client has worked in the same job for longer than this, the information would automatically be picked up during the initial exploration of the job). In order to become familiar with all the client's important work experience prior to this period, the practitioner can ask the client to list other jobs held and then ask if any of these others are jobs that the client really liked and/or are similar to jobs the client would be interested in at a future date.

There are some psychiatrically disabled clients whose educational and work history has been so restricted that they lack any background data from which to engage in career exploration. They are unable to discuss work tasks, strengths and deficits, likes and dislikes because of an almost total lack of recent stimulation in these areas. One of their major deficits is an inability to explore career-related activities. Clients with this particular deficit might first gain some experience in a variety of sheltered workshop tasks before beginning their career exploration in earnest.

An example of a completed work experience summary form is presented in Table 7. May is a young woman who was previously hospitalized. She has been working for over two years now but is beginning to reexperience some of her earlier symptoms. She feels the job is part of her problem and has decided to explore career alternatives.

Practice Situations

Using Table 6 as a guide, fill out a work experience summary form for your most recent job. Then practice by exploring the work experience of a client or a friend. As before, remember to overview what you are going to do and to respond to the content and/or feelings that the person presents in response to your questions.

EXPLORING GENERAL INTERESTS

Exploration of general interests focuses on two specific areas: (1) hobbies or nonvocational interests and (2) jobs that the client might find interesting. The first of these areas includes what the client enjoys

Table 7. Completed Summary Form for a Work Experience

Work Experience Summary

Job Title: Administrative Assistant

	Employer Name	Dates of Employment
1.	Peerless Management	2/74 to 5/76
2.	Hokey Toy Co.	11/71 to 8/73
3.		to

Major Duties and Responsibilities

1. Handled personal typing, shorthand, and dictation for personnel manager
2. Supervised general secretarial staff
3. Scheduled appointments
4. Paid invoices of outside agencies
5.

Special Areas of Interest

	Liked	Reason		Disliked	Reason
1.	Typing	Work on own	1.	Supervision	Handling all gripes
2.	Billing	Work on own, no pressure	2.	Appointments	Too much pressure
3.			3.		
4.			4.		
5.			5.		

Special Areas of Competence

	Asset	Reason		Deficit	Reason
1.	Typing Speed	Lots of practice	1.	Supervision	Hard to boss others
2.	Organization	My nature	2.	Shorthand	Lack skill, get flustered
3.	Punctuality	Emphasized by parents	3.		
4.			4.		
5.			5.		

doing in his or her spare time. The latter area involves the initial career alternatives the client has thought about, for whatever reason. Exploring these areas helps the practitioner to understand more about what the client would like to do. Again, it is important for the practitioner to understand not only the client's interests but also the reasons for these interests. It is particularly important to explore the reasons that particular jobs are perceived as interesting. Is it because of what the client thinks he or she might like about the job (e.g., being outdoors), or is it because of some external influence (e.g., "My sister told me I'd really like it")? This is important information because it will be used by the practitioner and the client to generate an initial list of client values. A client may well be interested in a particular job because of *someone else's* values. It is important for practitioner and client to be able to make that distinction. A possible format for recording the information is presented in Table 8. A completed example for a young man recently released from a veterans' hospital is shown in Table 9.

Practice Situations

Using the format of Table 8 as a guide, complete your own general interests form. Again, practice gathering appropriate background data with a client or a friend. Do not forget to overview the task you will be doing and to respond to the information you receive.

Table 8. Summary Form for Client General Interests

General Interest Summary

Hobbies

	Name	*Time*		*Reason Liked*
1.	_____		1.	_____
				_____
2.	_____		2.	_____
				_____

Jobs that I think might be interesting

	Name		*Reason*
1.	_____	1.	_____
			_____
2.	_____	2.	_____
			_____

Table 9. Completed Summary Form for General Interests

General Interest Summary
Hobbies

Name	Time		Reason Liked
1. Fishing	15 years	1.	Solitude, being outdoors, challenge
2.		2.	
3.		3.	
4.		4.	
5.		5.	

Jobs that I think might be interesting

Name		Reason
1. Forest ranger	1.	Outdoors, would be on my own
2. Truck driver	2.	Money, would be on my own
3. Policeman	3.	My uncle is one and he enjoys it
4.	4.	
5.	5.	

EXPLORING CAREER VALUES

Once the client's educational and work experiences have been explored, the next step is to explore the client's career values. "Career values" are those criteria that the client feels are important in selecting an occupation. A client's career values might include such considerations as salary, chance for advancement, and independence.

The first step in exploring values is to generate a list of the things that are important to the client. A simple step is to begin by reviewing with the client the educational experience, work experience, and general interest forms. Particular emphasis should be placed on the client's likes and dislikes. In this regard, it is important that all values be stated in the same manner. Therefore, negative values (dislikes) should be converted to positive values (likes). For example, if the client expressed a dislike of "getting dirty on a job," the positive value would be "cleanliness." It is also important the the values be specific enough to have some meaning. For example, the client may express the values of "wanting to feel satisfied" and "having good working conditions." The practitioner will want to follow up this type of statement to find out what would actually make the client "feel satisfied" and "have good working conditions." The practitioner might say to the client, "So you're saying that you want to work in a good atmosphere and feel good about what you do. But could you be more specific about what you think good working conditions are and the kinds of things you might do on a job that would make you feel satisfied?" The principle to remember here is that the practitioner will want to work with the client to develop a general idea of what a client *means* by a particular value.

It is also important for the practitioner to understand why the value is important to the client. For example, a client may say that independence is very important. The practitioner can respond, "You feel strongly that being independent is a significant thing. Could you help me understand why that is important to you?" The client might then say that people looking over his or her shoulder really makes him or her nervous. (Much of this information, of course, will be contained in the educational experience and work experience forms presented earlier.)

Examples of values and the reasons for each value that might be derived from the previous educational experience, work experience, and general interest forms (Tables 5, 7, and 9) are presented in Table 10. It should be noted that the client may not always clearly articulate the reason that something is important. This is not critical. The main thing is for the practitioner to develop a broader perspective on the client and to understand enough about the client's value to see if other values are involved. For example, if the client has said that money represents security, then "job security" may itself become a value.

Table 10. Values Derived from Experience Summary Forms

Source	Value	Reason
Harry's educational experience (Table 5)	Work with hands Work with motors	"It's what I do best." "Motors interest me."
May's work experience (Table 8)	Typing Independence Unpressured situations Structure	"I like to type." "I work better by myself." "I get nervous when pushed." "I like to know where I stand."
Young veteran's, general interests (Table 10)	Outdoors Isolation Money Sister's opinion	"I enjoy peace and beauty." "People bug me." "I like things I can buy with it." "I trust her."

Once the initial list of values has been developed using the client's educational and work experience as stimuli, the next step is to ask the client what other things she or he might consider important in choosing an occupation. It is important to remember that the values refer to the general occupation and are not tied to a particular job. For example, "degree of supervision" may well be a characteristic of the occupation, but a value such as "friendly foreman or boss" is clearly tied to a particular job rather than an occupation.

When the list of values has been developed, the third step is to organize the values. One effective classification scheme is to divide the listed values into physical, emotional-interpersonal, and intellectual values. *Physical values* refer to those things that affect physical well-being (e.g., activity level of the job, physical comfort, cleanliness, salary). *Emotional- interpersonal values* refer to those criteria that affect the way one relates to him/herself and others (e.g., degree of contact with other people, amount of supervision, amount of job security). *Intellectual values* refer to those things that affect one's mind (e.g., amount of repetition involved; chances for advancement; opportunities to use a particular intellectual skill such as calculating, writing, planning). The purpose of reorganizing the list of values into categories is twofold. First, it can help make the list of values more understandable and meaningful to the client. Second, and most importantly, the categorization process can stimulate client and practitioner to think of any possible physical, emotional, and/or intellectual values that they might have forgotten.

Table 11 illustrates how some of the values used as earlier examples might be classified. Knowing the reason for a value can often help the practitioner to know where to classify it. For example, the fact that Harry indicated an interest in working with motors (i.e., he found it intellectually stimulating) helps us to know that this is an intellectual value.

**Table 11. Values Classified by Physical, Emotional-
        Interpersonal, and Intellectual Categories**

PHYSICAL VALUES

Work with hands
Typing
Outdoors
Money

EMOTIONAL-INTERPERSONAL VALUES

Independence
Unpressured situations
Structure
Isolation

INTELLECTUAL VALUES

Work with motors

Once the values developed to this point have been organized, the practitioner needs to work with the client one more time to expand the client's values. Although the process of developing client values is time-consuming, it is critical because these values will be the basis on which the client will later make the career decision.

The value list can be expanded in a number of ways. For example, the client can be asked to identify the occupational values of family members or friends. People frequently hold values similar to those held by family or friends. Standardized tests such as the Strong Vocational Interest Blank, the Edwards Personal Preference Schedule, or the MMPI may help the practitioner to identify the client's occupational values.

Perhaps the simplest and most direct way to expand values is to check out the values the client has developed against a list of values that past experience has shown are important in selecting a career. The following are traditional career value categories:

I. **Physical Value Categories**

A. Personal appearance: how one dresses on the job, cleanliness, and so on

B. Physical working conditions: physical comfort due to temperature, odors, and so on, as well as such things as hours worked and the job's location

C. Physical activities: physical duties such as lifting, standing, working with hands

D. Salary and benefits: the amount of money made, insurance coverage, and so on

II. Emotional-Interpersonal Value Categories

A. Job security: how much income is guaranteed, probability, and so on

B. Emotional-interpersonal working conditions: structure, pressure, amount of supervision, amount of isolation

C. Emotional-interpersonal activities: amount of interaction with people; what one does with the people (e.g., help, persuade)

III. Intellectual Value Categories

A. Chance for advancement: opportunity to move to a higher level job and/or learn new skills

B. Supply and demand: number of openings and stiffness of competition (this often has implications for how long the individual must wait for a job or the size of the geographic area in which the search must be undertaken)

C. Intellectual activities: planning, decision making, computation, writing, training time, opportunities, and so on

This list is not meant to imply that every client will need to take into consideration one or more things in each category. Rather, the categories represent specific areas that the practitioner will want to explore with the client. It is frequently helpful to explore the client's living environment, as this will often have implications for developing occupational values. For example, for a client who values being with his or her family, a job that involves working evenings would be unfavorable. Thus, day-shift hours would become a job value.

In summary, then, the steps involved in developing a list of occupational values with reasons for those values are: (1) to review the educational experience, work experience, and general interest forms; (2) to review with the client any values she or he believes have been left out; (3) to organize the value list into physical, emotional-interpersonal, and intellectual value categories; and (4) to reexpand the value list using the traditional value areas as described above, plus life-style desires and other inventories or tests that the practitioner feels are appropriate for a particular client. Most clients will emerge from this process with a minimum of ten to twelve values to consider. Practitioners sometimes express concern that the career exploration process may falsely raise the hopes of the client. For example, a client may list job security and independence as career values, yet his or her work history and abilities may be so limited that the practitioner anticipates that few jobs will be available that will satisfy these values. Of course, later steps in the career counseling process introduce a healthy dose of reality. However, at this stage, the practitioner is attempting to explore the client's career from the *client's frame of reference*. If these values are important to the client, regardless of the client's ability to satisfy them to any extent, the information is important to the practitioner. It is far better that the practitioner and client be aware of these values early in the career counseling process rather than have them unexpectedly, or perhaps unknowingly, jeopardize the process at some later point.

In the understanding stage of career counseling, the meaning of these values to the client will be further clarified. At that time, specific definitions will be developed for each value, and the values will be further differentiated as to their relative importance to the client. The goal of the initial exploration of career values, however, is simply to identify what the client's values are.

An example of a client's career values is recorded in Table 12. Don is a young man who has been undergoing psychiatric treatment for about six months. He has had a severe drinking problem but is starting to get control of it. He is a high school graduate with an IQ in the high normal range. He has had a variety of jobs in factories and construction and has now come to the point where he would like to look into other career alternatives. The value list in Table 12 was developed by Don and the rehabilitation practitioner with whom he is working.

Table 12. Don's Career Values

Physical Values	*Reasons*
Comfortable temperature	"I'm tired of being too hot and too cold."
Local location	"My family and friends are here, and I don't want to move from the area."
Physically active work	"I get itchy if I stay in one place all the time."
Salary	"I want to be able to live comfortably."
Emotional-Interpersonal Values	*Reasons*
Security	"I don't want to have to worry about layoffs and seasons — I've had enough of that and I think it contributes to my drinking."
Independence	"I want to just be reliant on myself. That way I can pick friends, rather than be forced into a relationship because I have to do something with someone."
Helping people	"I need to feel like I'm doing something to benefit others."
Intellectual Values	*Reasons*
Chance for advancement	"I'd like to be able to see a future in the job."
Structure	"I want to know what is expected of me."
Preparation time	"I don't want to be going to school the rest of my life. I don't enjoy studying that much."

Practice Situations

As an initial practice step, develop a list of the physical, emotional-interpersonal, and intellectual values that are important to you. Record your values in a format similar to Table 13. When you have completed this exercise, practice with a client or a friend for whom the value exploration process would be relevant. It is especially important when going through the value exploration step to respond empathically to the client. This will ensure that you understand the client's value. Also, be sure to overview the value development steps you will be taking with the person, preferably in writing.

Table 13.   Sample Format for Developing Personal Career Values

Physical Values   *Reasons*

_____   _____

_____   _____

_____   _____

_____   _____

_____   _____

Emotional-Interpersonal Values   *Reasons*

_____   _____

_____   _____

_____   _____

_____   _____

Intellectual Values   *Reasons*

_____   _____

_____   _____

_____   _____

EXPLORING INFORMATION ABOUT THE CLIENT'S WORLD: A SUMMARY

Goal: To enable the client to identify specific and realistic job alternatives.

1. Overview the process with the client, preferably in writing.

2. Explore the client's educational experience by conducting a structured interview with the client.

    Gather educational information and explore the reasons for the client's likes, dislikes, aptitudes, and deficiencies.

3. Explore the client's work experience.

    Gather information about the client's previous job experience and explore the reasons for the client's likes, dislikes, aptitudes, and deficiencies.

4. Explore the client's general interests.

    Gather information about the areas of hobbies, nonvocational interests, and jobs that the client might find interesting.

5. Explore the client's career values.

    Generate an initial list of the things that are important to the client by using the client's educational and work experience and general interests as stimuli.

    Generate the reasons that the value is important to the client.

    Review with the client any additional career values.

    Organize the value list into physical, emotional-interpersonal, and intellectual value categories.

    Expand the value list by using traditional value areas, lifestyle decisions, and/or standardized tests.

6. Respond to the information presented by the client by responding to the client's feeling, content, or both.

EXPLORING HOW THE WORLD OF WORK IS ORGANIZED

Just as psychiatric rehabilitation clients resist exploring themselves, so they often resist exploring the world of work. The reasons are similar. Doubts exist about whether they can really make the efforts pay off. The clients often feel they will be lucky to get any job. Many times this will be voiced as "I'll take any job." The implication is that the client will be lucky to get anything at all — so why even look at options? Again, successful career counseling will involve the client in this exploration process. What the client does as an occupation will affect his or her life, both on and away from the job. Thus, even for lower-functioning clients, it is critical that the alternatives be examined.

EXPLORING WORK/INTEREST AREAS

The world of work can be an overwhelming concept. The *Dictionary of Occupational Titles* contains over 40,000 job titles. It is obviously impossible for the client to explore anything approaching this number of alternatives. Therefore, the client needs to identify a segment of the world of work to explore seriously. One strategy for identifying this segment is to use the client's own interests. Thus, the goals of this section are twofold. First, the client needs to understand how the world of work can be organized in terms of interests. Second, the client needs to decide which interest area to initially explore in greater detail. Many different systems have been developed for classifying jobs by interests (e.g., Holland, 1973; Super, 1957). Perhaps the most widely used is the "data/people/things" system developed as the foundation for the *Dictionary of Occupational Titles (DOT)*. This system will be used here. Each category, its definition, and some sample jobs are included in the following list:

Data Occupations

Data occupations stress working almost exclusively with data, in the form of words or numbers. There is very limited emphasis on interacting with people. If equipment is used at all, it is used simply as a means to process data. Examples in this area would include typists, meter readers, bookkeepers, computer programmers, accountants, and economists.

People Occupations

People occupations stress working almost exclusively with people, usually in a service or helping role. The worker uses almost no equipment (things) or information (data). Examples in this area would include waiters/waitresses, security officers, service station attendants, models, and flight attendants.

Things Occupations

Things occupations stress working almost exclusively with tools and equipment. Little or no interaction with people is required. Little data is used in performing the job. Examples in this area include factory assemblers, long-distance truck drivers, welders, heavy-machinery operators, and meat cutters.

Data/People Occupations

Data/people occupations require working with both data and people. Use of equipment is not central to performing the job. Examples from this area include telephone operators, receptionists, travel agents, department store or general salespersons, policemen, teachers, and counselors.

Data/Things Occupations

Data/things occupations require working both with written or numerical information and with tools and equipment. Interacting with other people is only a minimal job requirement. Examples from this area include various types of mechanics, carpenters, electricians, bricklayers, repair persons, dental technicians, engineers, chemists, and biologists.

People/Things Occupations

People/things occupations require working with both people and things. Determining or using information is minimal. Examples here would include such occupations as orderlies, nurse's aides, home attendants, veterinary assistants, and recreation leaders.

Data/People/Things Occupations

Data/people/things occupations require working with information, people, and tools and equipment as part of the job. Examples from this area would include cooks, photographers, automobile and parts salespersons, barbers and beauticians, dental hygienists, veterinarians, physicians, and nurses.

There is a certain amount of leeway in classifying a particular job. For example, it is almost impossible to say at which point a hospital orderly starts using enough information or equipment for the job to be categorized as "data/people" or "people/things," rather than just "people." It is entirely possible for occupations to be categorized in more than one area. The important thing is that the client understands the elements contained in the interest area and the job. The client may then classify the job according to the way that she or he experiences the predominance of the three elements. For lower-functioning clients, the practitioner may wish to categorize the job titles into only three categories: people, data, and things; or people, numbers, and machines.

The goal is for the client to understand how the world of work can be classified by personal interests. After the practitioner has explained an interest area to the client and has given some examples, a good check step is to see if the client can generate some examples in that area. After all categories have been explained, the client can try to categorize any jobs in which she or he has articulated a previous interest.

Practice Situations

Check yourself out at this point to see if you can generate at least four occupations in each interest area. Try to think of occupations that you could later use as good examples for the clients with whom you work. Use a format similar to Table 14. Then try to explain to a client or a friend how the world of work can be classified by worker interests. Have the person classify some examples of their own as a demonstration of their understanding.

IDENTIFYING PREFERRED WORK/INTEREST AREA

Once the client is familiar with the interest categories, the next step is to identify the preferred interest area. The practitioner can simply have the client explore the question, "Which of the interest categories *best* fits my values, the activities I have liked in my past work and educational experiences, and my general interests?" The category identified by the answer to this question is assigned the number 1. The practitioner might also wish to have the client identify his or her second and third choices as well.

In addition to the information that the client has generated about him/herself through exploration, the practitioner may also find it helpful to introduce interest tests as a means of helping the client to rank-order interest areas. The reasons for doing this range from client uncertainty about values or activities to conflicts among these different indicators to client need for confirmation that she or he has chosen the "right" thing. If interest tests are used, it can be emphasized that the test results are only additional information to be explored. The tests are not the sole determiner of the rank order of the client's interest areas.

In most cases there will be inconsistencies among the information collected. Thus, the client will want to look at the trend of the information developed and not become bogged down by the fact that there are inconsistencies in the interest patterns.

Table 14.   Sample Format for Generating Occupations by Interest Areas

Data   _____

                  _____

                  _____

                  _____

People   _____

                  _____

                  _____

                  _____

Things   _____

                  _____

                  _____

                  _____

Data/People   _____

                  _____

                  _____

                  _____

Data/Things   _____

                  _____

                  _____

                  _____

People/Things   _____

                  _____

                  _____

                  _____

Data/People/Things _____

                    _____

                    _____

                    _____

Don, the young man with the drinking problem, rank-ordered his top three areas of interest as follows:

1. Data/people/things
2. Data/things
3. Data/people

Practice Situations

As a practice exercise, you can rank-order your three most preferred interest areas. Once you have completed the interest-ranking exercise for yourself, practice with a client or a friend. Be sure to overview, preferably in written form, what you are going to do with the client or the friend to explore his or her interests. Also remember to respond to the content and/or feelings presented by the individual.

EXPLORING EDUCATIONAL REQUIREMENT CATEGORIES

Organizing the world of work by interests does not identify a specific enough portion of the world of work for the client to explore. Understanding how the world of work can be organized by educational requirements will help the client to identify a more specific segment of possible careers to explore. Introducing educational requirements as a method of organization will also help to bring a note of reality to the exploration process. There are, then, two goals for this section: first, to have the client understand how the world of work can be organized by educational requirements; and second, to have the client decide which educational requirement level to initially explore.

As with interest areas, several strategies can be used to organize the world of work by requirements. The strategy employed in this book uses educational requirements to organize careers. Each category, its definitions and some sample occupations are included in the following list:

Educational Level 5

Occupations in this category require four years of college or graduate school training. Examples of occupations in this category include various types of scientists, teachers, registered nurses, doctors, and engineers.

Educational Level 4

Occupations in this category require two years of junior or community college training, or three or four years of apprenticeship. Examples of occupations in this category include computer programmers, policemen/policewomen, restaurant and hotel/motel managers, medical and legal secretaries, insurance agents, dental and x-ray technicians, carpenters and construction electricians, flights attendants, and recreation supervisors.

Educational Level 3

Occupations in this category require from six to twenty-three months of technical, vocational school, or apprenticeship training after high school. Examples of occupations in this category include bookkeepers, clerk-typists, bank tellers, long-distance operators, secretaries, various types of mechanics (e.g., air conditioning, diesel, refrigeration), draftsmen, heavy-equipment operators, and meat cutters.

Educational Level 2

Occupations in this category require a high school diploma or its equivalent and up to five months of training. Examples of occupations in this area include typists, meter readers, food store checkers, various retail salespersons, insurance claims clerks, receptionists, local truck drivers, mail carriers, and nurse's aides or orderlies.

Educational Level 1

Occupations in this category do not require a high school diploma or its equivalent. Example of occupations in this category include bartenders, waiters/waitresses, short-order cooks, stock clerks, service station attendants, factory assemblers, common laborers, and janitors.

As with interest areas, there is a certain amount of leeway in classifying a particular occupation by requirements. For example, some companies employing long-distance truck drivers may not require a high school diploma if the candidate can meet the other qualifications. The specifics depend on the local requirements and the level of supply and demand. Likewise, secretarial positions may be obtained directly from high school, particularly if the candidate has attended a vocational high school offering an office education program. Again, the key factor is for the clients to know that there are educational requirements, that the world of work can be organized in terms of these requirements, and that they can understand this organizational system.

The practitioner will want to follow the same procedures as were used in the organization-by-interests strategy to help the client to understand the organization by educational requirements. In particular, the practitioner can explain the educational levels to the client and give some examples. The practitioner may then check the client out by having the client generate examples of occupations at each educational level in his or her area of interest. The client may also categorize the educational level of any occupations in which she or he has indicated an interest. Table 15 shows an example of occupations at each level of education in Don's interest area of "data/people/things."

Table 15. Occupations Identified by Educational Levels

Interest Area:	*Data/People/Things*
Educational Level 5	Dentist
	Physical therapist
Educational Level 4	X-ray technician
	Funeral director
Educational Level 3	Inhalation therapist
	Medical laboratory assistant
Educational Level 2	Cook/chef
	Local bus driver
Educational Level 1	Taxi driver
	Short-order cook

Practice Situations

You can now check yourself out by generating at least two occupations at each level of education in your particular area of interest. Use a format similar to Table 16.

Table 16. Sample Format for Developing Occupations by Educational Levels

Interest Area: _____

Educational Level 5 _____

_____

Educational Level 4 _____

_____

Educational Level 3 _____

_____

Educational Level 2 _____

_____

Educational Level 1 _____

_____

IDENTIFYING PREFERRED EDUCATIONAL REQUIREMENT CATEGORY

Once the educational requirement levels have been learned by the client, the next step is to identify the level of education the client is most likely to attain. In other words, the practitioner will want to help the client ask and answer the question, "How much more training am I willing and able to attain?" In part, this exploration can be based on discussions with the client of past educational achievement and aspirations. In addition, general and/or specific aptitude tests may be helpful at this point. They will help clients to understand both the general educational level they can expect to achieve and specific occupations within an educational level for which they have the required aptitudes. In Don's case, he and the practitioner identified level 3, high school plus at least six months training, as a realistic educational level.

Practice Situations

At this point, you can practice exploring educational levels with a client or a friend. To do this, you will want to overview in writing with the client the steps you will be taking. Then, explain the educational-level definitions, give some examples at each level, and work with the individual to develop at least two examples at each level. Finally, if appropriate, use further discussion and testing to determine the educational level at which the client is going to explore occupations.

During this process, it is critical that you respond to the feelings and/or content presented by the individual. Clients may well have had many fantasies about what they would like to achieve in their lives. Determining a realistic educational level to explore can be a rude shock, but a realistic level of education expectation must be developed. This is obviously one key to success or failure.

It is ultimately the client who will make the decision about the educational level that she or he will try to attain. A practitioner can introduce as much information as possible into the discussion and raise any objections to the client's chosen level. The practitioner may arrange for the client to obtain additional information about his or her decision by observing the activities of various educational settings and talking with students in these settings. However, if the client ultimately decides on a level different from the one the practitioner feels is best, either above it or below it, then the practitioner's responsibility is (1) to do everything possible to help the client succeed and/or (2) to be available at a later date to assist in whatever changes need to be made if the client's goal proves to be unattainable. It is important to remember that rehabilitation is still more an art than an exact science. Although practitioners have wisdom and instruments, their predictions may sometimes be less than perfect.

EXPANDING THE NUMBER OF REALISTIC OCCUPATIONAL ALTERNATIVES

Now that the practitioner has worked with the client to identify a specific interest area and educational level to explore, it is time to begin to expand the occupational alternatives. In particular, the practitioner will want to work with the client to identify a minimum of five to ten occupational alternatives. In other words, practitioner and client try to develop a list of occupations that will meet the client's values. There are a variety of sources for the practitioner and client to utilize to develop the list of occupations. These may be roughly categorized into *people* sources and *things* sources. People sources include professionals in the field of occupational information, people who work in the work category, and, of course, the client and the practitioner. *Things* are represented by such sources of information as books (e.g., *Occupational Outlook Handbook*), pamphlets (e.g., *Occupational Briefs*), employment service microfiche, and interest and aptitude tests.

Table 17 is an example of the occupational possibilities developed for Don within the level 3 educational requirement and the data/people/things interest area. These activities were generated by the practitioner and Don, using the *Occupational Outlook Handbook (OOH)* as a resource. It is important that the practitioner try to include occupational possibilities for which future job openings will exist. Various government pamphlets, such as the *OOH*, are helpful in keeping the practitioner's information on job trends as up to date as possible.

Table 17. Don's Career Alternatives

Interest Area:	People/Data/Things
Educational Level Level 3	Career Alternatives

1. Barber

2. Dental assistant

3. Licensed practical nurse

4. Surgical technician

5. Medical lab, assistant

6. Inhalation therapist

Often, it is not possible to generate occupations in the specific-interest-by-education cell that interest the client and that represent real possibilities for future employment. In this case, the practitioner has two alternatives. She or he can explore occupations in the same interest area with the client but at a level lower or higher in education; or the practitioner and the client can look at the next-best-liked interest area at the same educational level. This lack-of-occupations phenomenon is especially likely to occur in relation to people jobs. Relatively few jobs involve working with only people; many require working with data and/or things in addition to people. Therefore, if the client's interest area is "people," it may be necessary to search data/people or people/things jobs that emphasize the people component. Particularly at higher educational levels, things jobs also require working with data and/or people.

A thorough, structured client exploration process can be lengthy. In general, however, it can be an efficient use of practitioner time. It is the foundation from which career decisions are made *that often affect the remainder of the client's life and that may impact on the client's functioning in all major areas.* Viewed within that context, it may seem a legitimate use of time. In addition, a comprehensive, systematic career exploration process can serve to promote the client's involvement in the career counseling process. The career exploration tasks are concrete, yet designed to elicit the client's thoughts and feelings about past, present, and future career activities. The practitioner's deliberate attempts to demonstrate his or her understanding of the client's perspective further encourages client exploration. Yet, if the exploration process becomes too lengthy, the skilled practitioner can identify, based on his or her understanding of the total career counseling process, what tasks it would be best to modify or eliminate.

Practice Situations

As a practice exercise, try to generate five to ten occupational alternatives for your area of interest and your level of education. Remember, you can use your next-most-liked interest area or the next-closest educational level if necessary. Once you have practiced with yourself, you can practice developing alternatives with a client or a friend. Use a format similar to Table 18. As indicated in the previous sections, remember to overview what you are going to do and to respond to the client's reactions.

EXPLORING HOW THE WORLD OF WORK IS ORGANIZED: A SUMMARY

Goal: To enable the client to identify a specific segment of the world of work to seriously explore.

1. Overview the exploration process with the client.

2. Explore work/interest areas.

   Help the client to understand how the world of work can be organized in terms of interests.

3. Identify preferred work/interest areas.

   Help the client to determine the interest area that best suits his or her values, activities, past work and educational experience, and general interests.

   Help the client to rank-order the interest area.

4. Explore the educational requirement categories.

   Help the client to understand how the world of work can be organized in terms of educational requirements.

5. Identify the preferred educational requirement category.

   Help the client to ascertain the amount of training she or he is willing and able to attain.

6. Expand the number of realistic occupational alternatives.

7. Respond to the client's reactions by responding to his or her feeling, content, or both.

Table 18.   Sample Format for Developing Career Alternatives

Interest Area: _____

Educational Level	Career Alternatives
	1. _____
	2. _____
	3. _____
	4. _____
	5. _____
	6. _____
	7. _____
	8. _____
	9. _____
	10. _____

EXPLORING CAREER ALTERNATIVES: A SKILLED APPROACH

"Right now I guess you feel kind of nervous because you don't know whether you're going to be able to find any decent job for yourself," Sara told Jim, responding to the young man's obvious anxiety. His quick look and the tentative beginnings of a smile told her she'd hit the mark. *"Well, the most important thing we have to do is take it slow. To begin with, let's find out where you are right now in terms of your background and interests. That way, we can figure out the best place for you to go."*

Jim was more than ready to explore his background with Sara. After overviewing the procedure with him, Sara began to gather information about Jim's educational background. It turned out that he had begun a business program at the local community college but had dropped out at the end of the first semester.

"I had to work part-time, and it was just getting to be too much. It would've taken me two years to finish the whole program."

"You really felt overwhelmed and didn't think you could go the whole distance," Sara responded. *"Tell me, what sort of business courses were you concentrating on?"*

"Well — just general stuff, really. But if I had hung on, I would've gotten into some good computer courses. That's what really interested me!"

40

Sara went over Jim's high school record and learned that he had done quite well in several math and science courses. Then, having gathered enough data to complete his educational summary, she recycled the exploratory procedures for Jim's work background. He had held a number of summer and part-time jobs, but the only one he had really liked was a job with a vending machine company.

"That was OK," Jim told her. "I really liked being able to go out on my own, just check the machines, and make some simple repairs. I could just do everything on my own without anyone around to hassle me."

Once Jim's work summary was complete, Sara helped him explore his interests and hobbies — he enjoyed helping out friends by doing simple electrical repairs — and then explained to him how all of the information he had volunteered suggested a number of important personal values.

"You like to work on your own, independently," she said. "You like to work with machinery, especially electrical stuff."

"For sure!" Jim agreed enthusiastically. "Listen, when you do that kind of work you always know right where you are. There's never any confusion!"

Together, Sara and Jim arranged the latter's values in physical, emotional-interpersonal, and intellectual categories. Then Sara explained how Jim could organize his approach to the world of work. His rank ordering of his areas of interest served to confirm his top priority as a job in the data/things category. Finally, Sara helped Jim to determine the educational level that he could realistically expect to achieve.

"I really would like to finish the two-year college thing," Jim told her. "Only — well, maybe in something more specialized than just general business." They set his eventual educational level at level 3. Having done this, they were ready to begin listing some specific jobs that fit in with Jim's area of greatest interest — data/things — and his eventual level of education — two years of college.

"You know something? I really like doing things this way," Jim said as they were nearing the end of this exploratory phase of things. "It's better than — than just winging it. It really helps me know what my options are!"

Sara grinned and nodded. "It feels good to know that you can approach a problem systematically when you have to. And it also gives you some confidence that you can actually get where you want to go."

Chapter 3 UNDERSTANDING CAREER ALTERNATIVES

UNDERSTANDING CAREER ALTERNATIVES: AN UNSKILLED APPROACH

It wasn't that Marion was totally without skills. She was fully aware of how important it was for a client to explore career options. The problem was that she felt exploration alone was sufficient.

There was no doubt she had helped Ernie Dominguez. At the start of their session he had been totally adrift, totally without direction. Helping him to explore his background and interests, Marion had found that Ernie loved to work outdoors. Further exploration revealed a good deal of information about his other interests as well as about his educational and work background. Marion was pleased with the way she could show Ernie how the information he had come up with fit into a specific area of interest and a specific level of education.

"Hey ... " Fascinated, Ernie had gazed down at the scratch pad on which Marion had been writing. "Hey, that's me, huh? I'm a people/ things guy! And a — what is it? — a level 2, huh? Wow, I never knew any of that before."

Marion always enjoyed the way clients reacted to her introduction of systematic interest and educational categories. It often seemed to them like magic of some sort — which was silly, of course. The real magic involved getting clients to act on the results of their exploration!

And this, it turned out, was exactly the sort of magic that was missing in Ernie's case. She helped him list four different career possibilities that fit into his interest and educational categories. One of these, a job with a landscaping firm, seemed perfect to Marion, and she told Ernie so.

"Landscaping, huh?" He looked at Marion, then down at the scratch pad again. "Huh, I never thought about that." For a moment he looked puzzled. Then he seemed to shrug this mood off. "Well, what do I know? I guess I can't argue with the facts."

Encouraged, Marion listed some contacts he could make in order to find out about jobs with landscapers. Ernie accepted all of this passively, almost as though he were willing his own doubts away. Leaving, he thanked Marion profusely. For her own part, she spent a silent moment hoping that the magic of effective action would strike Ernie and bring him success.

Alas, it didn't turn out that way. Less than a month later, Marion ran into Ernie at a downtown gas station. He was pumping gas, his face an expressionless mask. At first she wasn't even sure he recognized her.

"Oh, yeah, Ms. Martin," he'd said at last. "How's it goin'?"

"Fine, Ernie, fine. But what about you? What about —?"

"That landscaping thing?" Ernie had shrugged. "Ah, no one wanted to hear from me. Maybe it wasn't my thing, anyway. This job's OK for a month or two, anyway."

"And — and then?"

"I dunno — I was thinking maybe of going out to the Coast. Getting out of here, anyway. There's nothing around here for me."

And the thing that hurt, the thing that Marion thought of now as she sat in her office alone, was the way in which Ernie's expression had included her in the "nothing" that made up his life!

As we have seen, the clients' general knowledge deficits about themselves and the world of work may be overcome by exploration. However, clients may also lack the ability to make a systematic decision about which specific occupation to enter. This problem can arise for several reasons. First, the clients may not *understand what is important to them.* That is, the clients may not know what they want from a career so that they can use this information to evaluate occupational alternatives. Second, the clients may not *understand their occupational alternatives.* Third, although the clients may have all the information they need, they may not have a *systematic decision-making method* for using this information to make the choice. The result of any or all of these deficits is the inability to choose one occupation with which the client will feel satisfied.

As suggested in the previous chapter, it is unlikely that the client or a referral agency will state deficits in the manner previously described. The following are some typical problems that suggest these deficits:

I. The client presents several definite alternatives but indicates an inability to make a choice. Probing by the practitioner shows that the client

    A. can articulate what is important to him or her in choosing a career (i.e., his or her values) but can only vaguely describe what the values really mean or how much of the value needs to be attained to satisfy him or her;

    B. has only a limited amount of information about the occupational alternatives in which she or he is interested.

II. The client presents a tentative occupational choice, but the client (or the practitioner) is unsure as to whether it is the right decision. Again, probing by the practitioner reveals that the client has limited understanding of his or her values and/or the chosen occupation or other possible occupations.

III. The client has sufficient information about his or her values and occupations, but probing indicates that she or he is unable to use all the information in selecting an alternative. That is, although the client has several definite criteria on which to make the choice, she or he is really using only one or two criteria to make the decision.

The specific content for handling each of these deficits is discussed in the remainder of this chapter. An overview of the skills involved is presented in Table 19.

Table 19.   Skills of Understanding Career Alternatives

I. UNDERSTANDING THE CLIENT'S UNIQUE CAREER VALUES

A. Defining career values

B. Scaling career values

C. Weighing career values

II. UNDERSTANDING THE WORLD OF WORK IN RELATION TO THE CLIENT'S CAREER VALUES

A. Investigating specific occupational alternatives

B. Making career decisions using values/occupational knowledge

C. Developing new understanding through an internship experience

UNDERSTANDING THE CLIENT'S UNIQUE VALUE SYSTEM

Psychiatric rehabilitation clients are often very vague when they discuss themselves. Many are either uncomfortable talking about themselves or unable to be very detailed in their exploration. The self-exploration of such clients often uses a shorthand language where one idea covers many details. If clients are to make a successful career choice, it is necessary that they understand themselves in detail. More specifically, they need to understand or clarify the values important to them in making a career choice.

The process of understanding career values is a difficult step for many psychiatrically disabled clients. Often a career choice is made with only a vague idea of what the client's values are, what they mean to the client, and their relative importance. The understanding stage of career counseling is structured so as to help clients to develop as thorough an understanding of their career values as is possible. The steps involved in this phase are designed to maximize the client's understanding of what is involved in making a career choice. The amount of independent effort will obviously vary with different clients. However, even lower-functioning clients can be guided through the process. Even though these clients would not be able to replicate the career counseling process on their own, the career decisions they make will at a minimum more closely reflect their own values. Thus, although they may not completely comprehend the process, the possibility of career decisions being more satisfying to them will have been improved.

DEFINING OCCUPATIONAL VALUES

Defining the client's occupational values is a career counseling skill that can be applied to the client who has been able to develop a comprehensive list of values to consider in choosing a career but who remains unclear about what those values really mean to her or him. The practitioner needs to work with the client to help clarify those values. The first step is to help the client to define what each of the identified values really means. This is necessary because the same value may well mean different things to different people. For one person, the value "independence" may refer to the amount of time working with no supervision. To a second person, "independence" may mean the amount of time working on the job alone, with neither supervisors nor peers. Thus, the practitioner will want to make sure that she or he has a clear understanding of what the client means by a particular value. In addition, this type of classification provides the client with an opportunity to think through exactly what a particular value means to him or her.

Defining a value means specifying what the value means in operational terms. To operationalize something is to define it in an observable and measurable (i.e., behavioral) way. To define a value *observably* means to describe it in such a way that it can be experienced by one of the five senses. To *measure* a value means to attach a numerical value to the observable behavior. The basic strategy for measuring an observable behavior involves using *time* and *amount* to define it. Formats that can be used to do this are: (1) amount of _____, or (2) amount or percentage of time doing _____. For example, "salary" may be defined as "the amount of money I make each year." A "structured job" may be defined by the "amount of time spent doing tasks for which there are clearly defined procedures."

In clarifying values, it often turns out that what initially appeared to be a single value may in fact be made up of two or more values. For example, a client may express a desire to be comfortable at work. In working to find out what the client means by this value, the practitioner might discover that "comfort" refers to the temperature, the cleanliness of the atmosphere, and being able to sit. Thus, one value has become three — temperature, atmosphere, and sitting. Each of these values may then be defined:

Temperature: amount of time spent in place with temperatures above 50 degrees and under 80 degrees

Atmosphere: amount of time spent in an atmosphere that does not smell, sting the eyes, or have known physical danger

Sitting: amount of time spent sitting on the job

The check step, then, for knowing when a value has been defined is to make sure that it contains only one major element. Table 20 illustrates the values that Don and the rehabilitation practitioner operationalized.

Table 20. Don's Operationalized Values

Physical Values	*Definition*
Comfortable temperature	The amount of time I spend in places that are between 50° and 75°
Local location	The number of employers within a 20-mile radius of my home
Physically active work	The amount of time I am on my feet and moving, not sitting in one place
Salary	The amount of money I can make each year

Emotional-Interpersonal Values	*Definition*
Job security	The number of weeks I would be able to be employed
Independence	The percentage of time spent working on tasks or projects by myself
Helping people	The percentage of time spent doing tasks that directly benefit another person

Intellectual Values	*Definition*
Chance for advancement	The number of alternatives to which I can advance with no further formal training
Structure	The percentage of time spent doing tasks for which there are specific procedures
Preparation time	The amount of time needed for training before I can work in the field

47

Practice Situations

Practice operationalizing each of the values that you developed previously. Use a form similar to that illustrated in Table 21. You may, of course, add new values if the process of clarification stimulates new criteria. When you have completed this exercise, work again with a client or a friend to operationalize his or her values. Be sure to explain the method of operationalizing fully so that the person can actively participate in the process. Responding to the client's statements is critical to ensure that you accurately understand the client's value definition.

Table 21.   Sample Format for Operationalizing Values

Physical Values   *Definition*

_____   _____

_____   _____

_____   _____

Emotional-Interpersonal Values   *Definition*

_____   _____

_____   _____

_____   _____

Intellectual Values   *Definition*

_____   _____

_____   _____

_____   _____

SCALING OCCUPATIONAL VALUES

Once values have been defined, the second step in the clarification process is to develop favorability scales for each value. These are five-point scales that indicate the points at which the quantity of the value becomes very favorable, favorable, acceptable, unfavorable, or very unfavorable.

Below is an example of a favorability scale for salary.

Level 5 (very favorable): $12,000/year or more

Level 4 (favorable): $ 9,000/year to $11,999/year

Level 3 (acceptable): $ 7,500/year to $ 8,999/year

Level 2 (unfavorable): $ 6,500/year to $ 7,499/year

Level 1 (very unfavorable): $ 6,499/year or less

Developing favorability scales will help practitioner and client to understand the value in enough detail so that the value can be used to evaluate occupational alternatives.

In order to develop the scales, the practitioner will want to help the client to explore and understand three types of questions:

1. What amount of this value would you consider yourself fortunate to attain? Describe what it would be like if you had everything you wanted in terms of this value.

2. What amount of this value would you consider intolerable?

3. What amount of this value would you consider at least adequate for your needs?

The first question addresses level 5 of the value, the second question addresses level 1, and the third question level 3. Levels 2 and 4 simply fill in the gaps. For most clients, the order in which the questions are listed is the same order in which the questions can be asked. However, if a particular client finds that a different order is easier, the practitioner may vary the sequence.

Several other aspects of the scales need mention. First, as indicated in the "salary" example, the various points on the scale do not have to be made up of a single quantity. Rather, the points can contain a range of quantities of the value (e.g., $6,000-$7,500). Second, the scale points do not have to be the same size. Again, this is illustrated in the "salary" example. Level 4 covers a range of $3,000 per year while level 2 covers a range of only $1,000. Third, all points on the scale do not have to contain an amount. This is generally the case where the client does not experience five different quantities of the value as being really different to her or him. At the extreme, there may be only two points. For example, suppose a client feels that she or he absolutely did not want to work in an atmosphere that was polluted in any way (i.e., odorous, stinging to the eyes, or known to be physically dangerous). The favorability scale might then look like this:

Level 5: 100% of the time in a clean atmosphere

Level 4:

Level 3:

Level 2:

Level 1: Less than 100% of the time in a clean atmosphere

The scales should ultimately reflect the client's experience of the value. In this regard, it is important that the practitioner help the client to explore and understand the rationale for each point in the scale. The client cannot be allowed to say that "$25,000 per year" or "no supervision" would be very favorable situations without being asked to discuss his or her rationale. The practitioner can then add his or her perspective; but again, because the client will be the one to live with the decision, the scales reflect the client's perspective.

Variations in the scaling procedure can also be made when it is too complex for a client to understand. The scales could be described as two-point scales, with level 2 the minimal or adequate level and level 1 anything less than that. In other words, level 2 is considered to be OK and level 1 is less than OK. For example, a client might define the value of close supervision as the percentage of time a supervisor is available to answer questions. The two-point scale for that particular value could be "100% of the time is OK, and less than 100% is not OK." For lower-functioning clients, it may be more effective to use a two-point or perhaps a three-point scale (level 3 = great, level 2 = OK, level 1 = not OK). The examples in this text illustrate the more complex (and more accurate) five-point favorability scales. Simplifications of this scaling procedure can be made to improve client understanding. The five-point favorability scales for Don's values are shown in Table 22.

Table 22. Favorability Scales for Each of Don's Values

Physical Values	*Measurement*
Comfortable temperature	5 — 90% to 100% of time in places 50° to 75° 4 3 — 75% to 90% of time in places 50° to 75° 2 1 — Less than 75% of time in places 50° to 75°
Local location	5 — More than 20 employers within 20 miles 4 3 — 10-15 employers within 20 miles 2 1 — 5 or less employers within 20 miles
Physically active work	5 — Moving half the time or more 4 3 — Moving a third of the time 2 1 — Moving a quarter of the time or less
Salary	5 — $15,000 or more per year 4 3 — $7,500 to $10,000 per year 2 1 — Less than $7,500 per year

Emotional-Interpersonal Values	*Measurement*
Security	5 — 52 weeks 4 3 2 1 — Less than 52 weeks
Independence	5 — 75% of the time or more on own 4 3 — 50% to 75% of the time on own 2 1 — Less than 50% of the time on own
Helping people	5 — 50% of the time or more directly helping people 4 3 — 25% to 33% of the time directly helping people 2 1.— Less than 10% of the time directly helping people

Intellectual Values	*Measurement*
Chance for advancement	5 — 3 alternatives for advancement 4 3 — 1 alternative for advancement 2 1 — 0 alternatives for advancement
Structure	5 — 75% or more of time in structured tasks 4 3 — 40% to 60% of time in structured tasks 2 1 — Less than 33% of time in structured tasks
Preparation time	5 — Start immediately by on-the-job training 4 3 — 1 year academic training 2 1 — More than 1 year academic training

Practice Situations

Use the scales developed for Don's values as a guideline in developing favorability scales for each of your own values. Record your values in a format similar to Table 23. Again, after you have practiced developing scales for your own values, practice by developing favorability scales for the values of a friend or a client. Overview the steps (i.e., ask the three basic questions) and respond to the feelings and/or content that you receive in the answers to the questions. Do not forget to explore with the client *why* she or he feels the need for a certain quantity of the value.

Table 23. Sample Format for Developing Favorability Scales

Value	*Measurement*
_____	_____
	_____
	_____
_____	_____
	_____
	_____
_____	_____
	_____
	_____
_____	_____
	_____
	_____
_____	_____
	_____
	_____
_____	_____
	_____
	_____

WEIGHING OCCUPATIONAL VALUES

The final step in understanding the client's values is to weigh them according to their importance to the client. This is necessary because values vary in their importance to the client, a fact that must be taken into consideration in making any career decision.

The scale used to weigh values is as follows:

10 Most important value

9

8 More important values

7

6

5 Average-importance values

4

3 Less important value

2

1 Least important value

This scale is a *relative* scale. That is, although all values may be very significant for the client, some are relatively more important than others. The practitioner will want to begin the weighing process by having the client explore the question, "Which value is *most* important to me?" The value that best answers the question is rated 10. The process is then reversed. The client explores the question, "Which value is *least* important to me?" This value is rated 1. The practitioner then continues to alternate these questions for the remaining values. It is important to spread the weights so that the weights actually reflect the differing degrees of importance. If possible, half of the remaining values should be rated from 6 to 9, and the other half from 2 to 5. An example of Don's weighted values is shown in Table 24.

Table 24. Don's Weighted Values

Physical Values	Weights
Comfortable temperature	1
Local location	10
Physically active work	7
Salary	9
Emotional-Interpersonal Values	*Weights*
Security	8
Independence	2
Helping people	6
Intellectual Values	*Weights*
Chance for advancement	5
Structure	3
Preparation Time	4

As has been mentioned previously, some clients lack prior career experiences from which values can be generated. Others may be helped to generate values but may experience real difficulty in following the process of defining, scaling, or weighing values. Yet, becoming even minimally involved in these steps is helpful in selecting the most satisfying job. Once again, work samples, sheltered workshop tasks, volunteer positions, and internships are all methods of giving the client the opportunity to experience a particular activity. Then practitioner and client can develop an understanding of the client's values from a list of concrete likes and dislikes in relation to the activities experienced. The concept of developing an intern experience is further discussed later in this chapter.

Practice Situations

Follow the practice sequence typically used. First, weigh your own occupational values in a chart similar to Table 25, and then work with a client or a friend to weigh his or her values. Again, it will be important to respond to the client in order to assign accurate weights and to gain an understanding of the rationale for the weights.

Table 25. Sample Format for Weighing Values

Physical Values	Weights

Emotional-Interpersonal Values	Weights

Intellectual Values	Weights

UNDERSTANDING THE CLIENT'S UNIQUE VALUE SYSTEM: A SUMMARY

Goal: To facilitate the client's ability to make a successful career choice by helping the client to understand or clarify his or her values.

1. Help the client to define his or her occupational values. Specify what the values mean in observable and measurable terms.
2. Develop favorability scales for each value.
3. Weigh the values according to their importance to the client.
4. Respond to the information presented by the client.

UNDERSTANDING THE WORLD OF WORK

Even when psychiatrically disabled clients understand their values, they often lack information about occupational alternatives. They usually know a few of the activities involved in an occupation and perhaps something about working conditions, but other information is often missing (e.g., chances for advancement, personal qualifications, salary range). In addition, much of the information possessed is general rather than specific in nature. For example, the client may know that an automobile assembly line polisher finishes surfaces but may not have specific information about the kind of equipment used in this operation. This lack of specific information makes it difficult to accurately evaluate an occupation.

INVESTIGATING SPECIFIC OCCUPATIONAL ALTERNATIVES

In the exploration phase, the practitioner helped the client to explore his or her values and the world of work. In the understanding phase, the practitioner continued to work with the client to facilitate the client's specific understanding of his or her values. Now, the practitioner will want to complete the parallel process for the working world by helping the client to understand the world of work in relation to his or her values. In particular, the client needs to develop a thorough knowledge of the occupations in which she or he is interested.

During the exploration phase, the practitioner may have helped the client to identify five or ten occupations. Now, the practitioner will want to help the client decide which of these alternatives to research thoroughly. As a general rule, at least three alternatives are researched initially. If the client and/or the practitioner desire to research more than this number, of course, this can be done. However, if it seems appropriate to narrow the occupations to be researched, this is best done by going to a source that can give the practitioner or the client a general overview of the activities, qualifications, and employment prospects for the job. It will be recalled that sources can be divided into people and things. For the preliminary overview research, a general source is most efficient. That is, if at all possible the source should be able to tell about more than one job. The *Occupational Outlook Handbook (OOH)* and the *Dictionary of Occupational Titles (DOT)* are two good general sources. Among people, good general resources are professional vocational counselors. Of course, it may sometimes be necessary to consult with a person in the field if the more general sources do not have the needed information. The general information gained from the overview can then be integrated with the client's existing knowledge of his or her values to allow a preliminary screening. Don, after doing his general research in the *Occupational Outlook Handbook* and discussing the results with his practitioner, decided to begin thorough research by looking at the occupations of licensed practical nurse, medical laboratory technician, and inhalation therapist.

Once the decision has been made, the next step is to focus on the questions to ask. The practitioner can accomplish this by following a 5-WH (who, what, why, when, where, plus how) questioning strategy. Table 26 outlines the basic question areas and some standard follow-up questions. The goal of the research is to learn how favorable each occupational alternative is in terms of the values developed by the client.

Table 26. Standard Career Research Questions

Basic Questions	Follow-up Questions
WHO does the work?	What are the educational or training requirements?
	What are the personal qualifications?
WHAT do they do?	What are the major tasks performed?
	How much time is spent on these different tasks?
WHY do they do it?	What is the salary?
	What are the opportunities for advancement?
WHEN and WHERE do they do it?	What types of employers do they work for?
	What are the working conditions?
HOW do you get to do it?	What is the supply and demand?
	Where can training be obtained?

The 5-WH questions will cover information about many of the client's values. These questions will also ask for information in areas where the client does not have values. Experience has shown that this information gives a good perspective of the job. The questions may not address all the issues that are important to the client. The client will have to develop personal questions to address those issues that are not covered. For example, Don did not notice questions that specifically addressed his need to know about local locations, physical activity level, security, independence, or structure. Therefore, he added these personal questions to his list (see Table 27).

Table 27. Don's Personal Questions

Basic Questions	Follow-up Questions
WHO does the work?	What are the educational or training requirements?
	What are the personal qualifications?
WHAT do they do?	What are the major tasks performed?
	How much time is spent on these different tasks?
Personal	How much time is spent doing tasks for which there are definite procedures?
WHY do they do it?	What is the salary?
	What are the opportunities for advancement?
Personal	How much of the time would I be laid off?
WHEN and WHERE do they do it?	What types of employers do they work for?
	What are the working conditions?
Personal	How much time are you on your feet and moving each day?
	How much time do you work on tasks independently?
	Where are the potential employers located?
HOW do you get to do it?	What is the supply and demand?
	Where can training be obtained?

Once questions have been developed, a way must be found to answer them. Once again, the people and things sources of information are critical. Table 28 contains a basic list of people and things sources. The practitioner will want to help the client identify specific sources that can be used to supply the answers to questions. The practitioner can then help the client to match his or her list of questions about each occupation with the specific informational source.

Table 28.   Basic People and Things Sources

People Sources	Things Sources
1. Counselors	1. Books about all occupations
2. Employment interviews	2. Books about specific occupations
3. People who work on the job	3. Pamphlets about occupations
4. People who work with people in the job	4. Microfiche information banks
5. Tour guides and public relations or personnel workers in the job area	5. Newspapers
6. Teachers in the field	6. Telephone books

If the source is an agency or person, the following information is necessary (examples of answers are given in parentheses).

1. *What* is the specific source? (Massachusetts State Employment Service Job Center.)

2. *Where* is it located? (253 Huntington Avenue.)

3. *Who* is the contact person — perferably name and position, but at least position? (Mr. Joe Callahan, Veterans Counselor.)

4. *How* can the person be contacted? (Phone 727-6320.)

5. *How* do you use the source? (Develop value questions, bring notebook and pencil or pen to record information.)

For a written source such as a newspaper, the only questions that usually need be answered are "What is the specific source?" and "How do you use the source?" Sometimes it may be necessary to answer the question, "How can the source be obtained?" If the client is to get the information, the practitioner will want to make sure that he or she is prepared to use the source. As suggested by the example, to use an employment counselor effectively the client needs to know what questions to ask and what to bring to record the information. The practitioner can prepare the client to use the source by explaining what to do, demonstrating how to do it, and then having the client practice doing it.

To the extent that they are available, people are often able to give more precise and local information. Table 29 illustrates the way the rehabilitation practitioner helped Don match his questions about licensed practical nurses with the specific sources of information.

Table 29. Don's List of Sources for Questions about Licensed Practical Nursing

Question	Source
Who does the work?	
What are the educational requirements?	*Occupational Outlook Handbook (OOH)* State Licensing Board, City Hall, 359 Chestnut St., 727-6145
What are the personal qualifications?	*Dictionary of Occupational Titles (DOT)*
What do they do?	
What are the major tasks performed?	*OOH;* Ms. Kramer, LPN, City Hospital, 727-7800
How much time is spent on the different tasks?	Ms. Kramer
Why do they do it?	
How much do you have to lift?	Ms. Kramer
How much time do you spend doing tasks for which there are definite procedures?	Ms. Kramer
What is the salary?	*OOH;* Ms. Kramer
What are the advancement opportunities?	*OOH;* Ms. Kramer
What are the chances of a layoff?	Ms. Kramer
When and where do they do it?	
What types of employers can you work for?	*OOH*
What are the working conditions?	*OOH;* Ms. Kramer
How much time on your feet?	Ms. Kramer
How much time doing independent tasks?	Ms. Kramer
Where are the employers located?	Phone book
How do you get to do it?	
What is the supply and demand?	Mr. Jones, State Employment Service, 253 Huntington Ave., 727-6320
Where can training be obtained?	Ms. Kramer

The final step in researching occupations is to find the answers to the questions. Whether the practitioner or the client acquires the information will depend on the particular client. As a general rule, the client is responsible for getting as much of the information as possible, perhaps enlisting friends and relatives to help with obtaining the information. Clients can often obtain a great deal of information independently of the practitioner. As a result, the information is more meaningful to the client.

Table 30 shows the information that Don was able to collect about the occupation of licensed practical nurse.

Table 30. Don's Information about Licensed Practical Nursing

Education and training	1 year of training in state-approved program; covers nursing concepts and principles, anatomy, physiology, medical-surgical nursing, administration, nutrition, first aid, community health.
Personal qualifications	Pass licensing exam. 17 or 18 years old. H.S. graduate. Good health, patience, dependability.
Major tasks and percentage of time at each	*Hospitals:* Bedside medical care (temperatures, blood pressure, etc.) — 60%; bedside hygiene (baths, etc.) — 30%; assisting R.N. and physician in examining patients and carrying out complex nursing procedures — 10%.
	Private Home: Medical care — 20%; hygiene — 20%; meals and other household chores — 60%.
	Offices: Preparing patients for exam and treatment — 20%; clerical and reception duties — 80%.
Total time on definite tasks	Almost 100% of time is spent in tasks for which there is a very definite procedure.
Salary	$6,700 average; paid holidays, vacations, health insurance, and pension common in hospitals.
Advancement opportunities	None without further training.
Layoff time	None.
Types of employers	Hospitals (about half people), nursing homes, clinics, sanitariums, other long-term facilities, doctors' offices, public health agencies, welfare organizations, private homes.
Working conditions	Indoor work, usually air-conditioned if in hospital.
Activity level	On feet and moving about 75% of time.
Independent work	Working on independent tasks 80% of time.
Employers in my location	5 hospitals, 12 nursing homes.
Supply and demand	Excellent. Right now over 50 openings are on file at this state employment office.
Places to get training	Public schools (vocational education or adult education), junior college, hospitals.

Collecting information about specific job alternatives once again introduces the "reality" component into the career counseling process, just as the selection of the preferred educational level did in the exploration phase. It is at this point that the client may begin to realize that he or she no longer wishes to consider certain jobs. The qualifications may be too stringent, the working conditions unappealing, the supply-and-demand prospects too poor. At this point, the client may wish to drop certain alternatives from consideration simply on the basis of some insights about the job that were stimulated by his or her investigation. Obviously, the client's own realization that a certain job alternative is unrealistic is preferable to the practitioner's attempt to persuade the client that he or she is being unrealistic. In addition, this reality is based on facts provided by sources other than the practitioner, thus reducing the likelihood that the practitioner will be forced into an adversary role with the client.

Practice Situations

As a practice exercise, you can determine the occupations you will personally research, develop your question list, identify the specific sources you will use for each occupation, and then research that occupation. Once your personal career research has been completed, take a client or a friend through the process. Overview the steps that will be involved. If people sources are to be used, it is also helpful to rehearse the interview process with the individual so that the person will be successful in getting the information from the source. You will also have to help the person decide whether a phone contact is appropriate or a personal visit is required.

Making Career Decisions Using Values/ Occupational Knowledge

Once clients have come to understand their values and the occupations in which they are interested, there is sufficient information to make an occupational decision. The practitioner guides the client through four steps to identify his or her preferred occupational alternatives (summarized in Table 31). An example of Don's completed decision-making matrix is given in Table 32. Although the completed matrix might appear complex, it is quite simple to complete. The values and value weights have been identified during earlier phases of the career counseling process; they are listed in the left-hand columns. Similarly, the potential job alternatives have previously been identified; they are listed across the top. All that needs to be determined is the potential effect of each occupation on each of the client's values. This estimate is accomplished during step 1. The other three steps use simple mathematical operations to arrive at a numerical representation of which occupation is potentially the most satisfying.

61

Table 31. Summary of the Decision-Making Method.

Step 1   Assign each occupational alternative a 1-to-5 rating on each value, based on an estimate of how well that occupation will satisfy each value. This estimate is derived from the information collected during the investigation of each alternative.

Step 2   Assign the occupation a score for each value. The score is obtained by multiplying the value weight (1 to 10) by the degree of favorability the occupation has for that value (1 to 5). This procedure enters the relative importance of each value into the process.

Step 3   Evaluate the occupation across all the values. This is done by totaling the individual value scores obtained by the occupation.

Step 4   Obtain an average favorability score for each occupation. This is done by dividing the total value score obtained in step 3 by the sum of the weights. If the average favorability score for a particular occupation is 5, then the occupation is very favorable; if it is 4, then the occupation is favorable; if it is 3, then the occupation is acceptable; 2 is unfavorable; and 1 is very unfavorable. In general, the occupation the client ultimately chooses should have an average favorability score of at least 3.75.

Modifications can be made in the decision-making method to simplify the process for lower-level-functioning clients. As mentioned previously, the five-point favorability scales can be shortened to two-point scales (i.e., "OK" and "not OK"). If a particular occupation satisfies a particular value, a 2 can be recorded in the appropriate cell; if the value will not be satisfied, a 1 can be recorded. This will greatly simplify the arithmetic of steps 2, 3, and 4. Another modification might be made by eliminating numbers entirely, completing step 1 by placing the appropriate number of check marks (or red stars) in the correct cell. The arithmetic involved in steps 2 and 3 could then reduce to simply counting up the total number of check marks for each occupation. The attempt to arrive at an average favorability score (step 4) could be eliminated, and the occupations could simply be compared to one another in step 3 by looking at the total number of check marks a particular alternative received.

Regardless of the particular modifications, the key component of the career decision-making process is step 1. That is, *the client evaluates each occupation using each of his or her differentially weighted values*. The development of information about the client's career values and the gathering of career information is irrelevant if the client has no method of putting these two sources of information together in a way that accurately reflects both the client's world and the world of work. A practitioner skilled in the process of career counseling ensures that this critical decision-making step will, in fact, occur.

Table 32. Don's Decision Making Matrix

Values	Weights	Licensed Practical Nurse Favorability	Score	Medical Technician Favorability	Score	Inhalation Therapist Favorability	Score
Temperature	1	5	5	5	5	5	5
Local location	10	4	40	4	40	4	40
Activity	7	5	35	1	7	5	35
Salary	9	1	9	2	18	4	36
Security	8	5	40	5	40	5	40
Independence	2	5	10	4	8	5	10
Helping people	6	5	30	1	6	5	30
Advancement	5	1	5	1	5	2	10
Structure	3	5	15	5	15	5	15
Preparation time	4	3	12	3	12	4	16
TOTAL SCORES	55		201		156		237

Preferred Occupation = Inhalation Therapist

Favorability check: 237 divided by 55 = average favorability score of 4.3

63

Practice Situations

Using the decision-making matrix in Table 32 as a guideline, evaluate your own career alternatives. Record your scores in a format similar to Table 33. Then, practice by taking a friend or a client through the decision-making process. Explain the four steps, and show an example of each. Then have the person use the process to make the decision under your supervision. If the preferred occupation has a score of less than 3.75, the practitioner will want to help the client reevaluate the situation. One way to do this, of course, is to try to find other occupations that will better fit the client's values. This may involve a reexamination of interests and educational levels. A second alternative is to try to develop strategies that will overcome the specific weaknesses in the occupation — particularly on those values that are heavily weighted. For example, one of the major problems for Don with the LPN job was the low salary. If this had been his preferred occupation, he might be able to overcome this deficit by working full-time at one job and part-time at another.

DEVELOPING NEW UNDERSTANDING THROUGH AN INTERNSHIP EXPERIENCE

Particularly when the client lacks real-life exposure to the selected job, it is very helpful for the practitioner to work with the client to develop an internship experience. An internship experience is one in which the client goes to the job and observes it intensely. The client may even try to do some of the tasks that require little or no training. The goal of the internship is to review the earlier decision. Thus, the client will want to use the experience to further understand his or her career values. In particular, the client will want to determine whether any values need to be added to the list and/or whether the weights need to be changed. For example, if Don had gone to a medical laboratory he might have discovered that the purity of the air as well as the temperature was an important part of his being comfortable. In addition to possible value changes, an internship also gives clients an opportunity to check out the information they have received. Based on new values and new data, the practitioner can then work with the clients to reevaluate their previous decisions.

Just as clients may use an internship experience to validate a decision, they can also use it prior to making the decision. That is, the internship can be used as a mechanism for investigating specific alternatives in hopes of gathering information about the job that is more detailed or more localized than would otherwise be available.

The format of the internship usually varies from a couple of hours to one or two full days. Its duration will depend upon the ability and/or willingness of the employer to provide any necessary supervision to the

Table 33. Sample Format for Making a Systematic Career Decision

Values	Weights	Favorability	Score	Favorability	Score	Favorability	Score

Total Scores: _____   _____   _____

Preferred Occupation = _____

Favorability check: $\dfrac{\text{(occupation score)}}{}$ divided by $\dfrac{}{\text{(sum wts.)}}$ = _____

65

client, the time necessary to learn about the job, and the time available to the client. The client may also wish to intern at the same job with several different employers, thus gaining a broader perspective on the occupation. This will be particularly important if it is the kind of job that varies considerably from employer to employer or is available in very different settings. For example, one can work as an LPN in a hospital, a nursing home, an office, or a private home.

Volunteer positions that can be used as internships often exist in the client's area of interest. The practitioner can be helpful by providing the client with information as to how to find out about the volunteer experiences that may be available. Some examples of possible volunteer activities are: tour guide in a museum, day-care assistant in a nursery, groundskeeper at a senior citizens' home, auto mechanic/teacher at a vocational school.

Depending on the abilities of the client, either the practitioner or the client can arrange the internship. In either case the arrangements should cover the following:

1. Purpose of the visit (e.g., to obtain information about the job by observation and questions so that the client can make a decision about whether or not to enter the field). It may be helpful to explain the career counseling process to this point so the employer knows that the client is serious about his or her occupational decision making.

2. Supervision of the client's visit.

3. Length of visit.

4. Arrangements for the client to meet the contact person.

If the business or agency is small, the initial contact can be made with the owner. If the business is large, the initial contact can be made with the local manager, the public relations department, or the personnel department. The practitioner skills involved in setting up an internship experience have been called community coordinating skills. These skills are covered in detail in Book 6 of this series.

UNDERSTANDING THE WORLD OF WORK:
A SUMMARY

Goal: To enable the client to accurately evaluate alternative occupations and choose a preferred occupation.

1. Select the occupational alternatives to research thoroughly. Overview the activities, qualifications, and prospects for a job, and integrate that information with the client's values to determine the desirability of obtaining more information about the job.

2. Use the 5-WH questioning strategy to gather information about the occupations.

3. Help the client to answer the questions by matching the questions to specific informational sources, making sure that the questions are adequately answered.

4. Assist the client with the decision-making matrix, helping the client rate each occupation for each differentially weighted value.

5. Help the client to assign each occupation a score for each value and evaluate the occupations across all the values.

6. Calculate the average favorability score for each occupation and make sure that the client's preferred occupation is favorable.

7. Arrange for an internship experience for those clients needing real-life exposure to the preferred occupation.

UNDERSTANDING CAREER ALTERNATIVES:
A SKILLED APPROACH

Sara had helped Jim develop a number of personal values related to his career options: for example, independence, specialized training, and specialized work.

"Great," she said. "Now we've got to pin these values down a bit more carefully." She overviewed the process of operationalizing values with Jim and then took him through the actual process. His value of "independence" really meant the amount of time Jim could actually spend working alone. "Specialized training" meant the number of courses he could take in a training program that would be directly applicable to his intended job. And "specialized work," of course, meant the number of specific technical tasks he would have to perform.

Next Sara took Jim through the procedures involved in developing a favorability scale. He caught on quickly and had soon developed a specific rating for each value. For his value of "independence," for example, level 5 (most favorable) turned out to be a job in which 90 to 100 percent of his work could be done alone, and level 1 (most unfavorable) was a job in which less than 25 percent of his work could be done alone.

Once Jim had worked out a favorability scale for each of his occupational values, Sara helped him to assign numerical weights to each value. On a 1–10 scale where 10 was "most important," Jim gave a full 10 to "independence" and lower relative weights to all his other values.

They were ready for the next phase of activity. Sara knew that although it was certainly important for Jim to understand himself and his own values it was equally important for him to gain an understanding of the specific nature of the career alternatives themselves. After all, how else could he see how his values fit with a particular job?

Sara and Jim had already developed a list of seven possible occupations that fit into the general categories of Jim's interests and educational background. Now they narrowed the original list of seven down to three: electrician, computer programmer, and x-ray technician. Each could be approached through a specialized training program. But before Jim could make an intelligent decision among the three, he had to gain additional information about all of them. Sara worked with him to develop a list of specific people and things sources of information. Calling the local technical school, for example, she was able to get Jim an appointment with several different teachers, each with a background in one of Jim's three possible career fields.

It was almost a week before Sara saw Jim again. But when he reappeared, he was carrying a notebook crammed with information. Now she was able to sit down with him and develop a matrix that would allow him to quantify the relationships between each job and each of his occupational values. Working with numbers and precise definitions, Jim was in his element. He confided to Sara his suspicion that the job as an electrician was going to come out on top. But it didn't. Given the primary importance he placed upon independence and the data he had unearthed about the inevitable subservience of apprentice electricians to their supervisors or foremen, this job finished second. His potentially most satisfying option turned out to be the career in computer programming.

"Huh!" Jim explaimed, looking at the results as his face broke into a huge grin. "How about that? I guess what made the difference was finding out how much freedom a good programmer has once he gets started — especially one who works for a relatively small company."

Sara answered his grin with one of her own. "It feels good to know just where you want to get to," she told him. "Now the only thing we have to do is figure out just how to get you there!"

Chapter 4 ACTING ON THE CLIENT'S CAREER CHOICE

ACTING ON THE CAREER CHOICE: AN UNSKILLED APPROACH

"Man, I wish all clients were this easy to take care of," Henry thought. And it was true — Darlene Johnson was nothing if not a go-getter with a real sense of purpose and drive.

Henry had spent a lot of time with Darlene. He had begun by helping her to explore her educational and work experience and her areas of interest. He had gone on to promote her understanding of her career alternatives in terms of her own values. In the end they had worked together to determine which of Darlene's career possibilities was really the best. And they had come up with a clear answer. Darlene's career choice was to work as a buyer for a department store.

"I'm glad the numbers came out that way," Darlene told him. "'Cause I had this feeling all along that's just where I want to be. I mean, I think I've got a natural flair for the work, you know. And now that I've — you know, solved my family problems — well, the sky's the limit!"

There was no doubting her enthusiasm. Henry continued to find it a pleasure to work with Darlene as they mapped out a plan of action designed to get her to her goal. Fortunately, one of the local branches of a large department store chain had an excellent training program for prospective buyers. And Darlene had previously worked as a salesperson in this same store — an important asset in qualifying her for the training program. Then, too, she looked the part: attractive, well-groomed, and quite articulate when she chose to be.

"You can do it, Darlene," Henry told her, sharing the enthusiasm she clearly felt. "All we have to do is make sure you take care of all the preliminary things you need to do to get into the program."

Working carefully, they planned Darlene's campaign. She would have to get a transcript from her old high school as well as letters of recommendation from previous employers — and expecially from her supervisor in the days when she had worked at the store.

"That's no problem," Darlene said confidently. "She and I are really good friends now. I know she'll recommend me."

And indeed, Darlene's friend came through — as did all the other people whom Darlene contacted for help. The day she was accepted into the buyer's training program she called Henry, her voice jubilant.

"I got it," she crowed. "It's in the bag! Listen, I can't thank you enough."

As it turned out, however, Darlene's thanks had come too soon. In the habit of following up on his clients, Henry called her at home one evening about two months later. The Darlene who answered the phone sounded like a different person: down, dejected, with barely enough energy to say hello.

"Well how's the program?" Henry asked.

"What program?" Darlene muttered something in a low voice. "They gave me the boot."

"What? They fired you? But why?"

"Well, see, I've always had this little problem about liking to take days off — you know, like when it's a really beautiful day and you just feel like going somewhere and having a good time? Only — only it turned out they couldn't handle it. I missed a couple days and then — wham! — the next think I know there's a note telling me I'm dropped from the program. Now I ask you, is taking a day off such a terrible thing?"

But Henry wasn't thinking about the relative merits of taking a day off. Instead, he could think of nothing but the fact that he had never bothered to find out about any problems like this that Darlene might have.

If only he had known! If only he had found out, they could have dealt with it!

If only ...

At times, the psychiatric rehabilitation client may come to the practitioner with a definite and realistically attainable goal. For most clients, however, having a goal is not enough. For a variety of reasons, the client may be unable to develop and implement a *plan of action* to reach that goal. The deficits that keep the client from reaching the goal can vary from a history of absenteeism to not knowing where to find an employer to not having the finances to pay for needed training. Thus, the practitioner will want to help the client to *develop* and *implement* a career plan.

ACTING TO DEVELOP A CAREER PLAN

A *career plan* is defined as those steps needed to take the client to the career goal. Essentially, this involves assessing potential problems and developing programs to overcome the problems. If the practitioner has developed a diagnostic plan in the early stages of the rehabilitation process, many of these problems will already have been identified. However, once the practitioner and the client have settled on a specific career goal, it is well to recheck the client's deficits in light of the goal and to add to the diagnostic picture previously completed.

Other books in this series have dealt extensively with the topics of problem assessment and program planning (Book 1: *The Skills of*

Diagnostic Planning, and Book 2: *The Skills of Rehabilitation Programming).* This chapter will summarize the skills involved and show their application to the development of a career plan. The skills are summarized in Table 34.

Table 34.   Skills of Acting on a Career Choice

I. ACTING TO DEVELOP A CAREER PLAN

    A. Identifying and categorizing problems

    B. Assessing present problem behavior

    C. Assessing the needed goal level

    D. Developing career steps to the needed goals

II. ACTING TO IMPLEMENT THE CAREER PLAN

    A. Specifying needed resources

    B. Assigning completion dates

IDENTIFYING AND CATEGORIZING PROBLEMS

The initial step in developing a career plan is to identify the problems that may interfere with the client's reaching his or her career goal. To develop this list of problems, the practitioner can begin by asking the client to identify the problems that might inhibit attainment of the career goals. Some ideas about what can be on this list probably were discussed during the exploration stage. Once this initial list has been developed, the next step is to examine all potential problem areas carefully. This can be accomplished by first exploring the physical, emotional-interpersonal, and intellectual deficits that the client may have. In other words, the practitioner will want to help the client categorize the problems already identified and then examine each area to see if any other problems exist.

For the purposes of this book, *physical* (P) deficits refer to those things that primarily involve performing some physical behavior. A deficit is categorized as *emotional-interpersonal* (E) if the primary behavior involves relating to other people or oneself. An *intellectual* (I) deficit is one in which the behavior primarily involves thinking or mental activity. Table 35 lists some examples of common PEI deficits that could interfere with clients achieving their career goals. Note that some behaviors may be more difficult to classify than others; they could fit into two or perhaps three categories. In these cases, the behavior may be placed in the category that has the most deficits; this "most deficient" area is probably playing a fundamental role in the client's problems.

Table 35. Common Client Deficits, Classified PEI

Physical	Emotional-Interpersonal	Intellectual
Lack of good grooming	Lack of temper control with boss or coworkers	Inability to follow directions
Obesity	Inability to make eye contact with others	Inability to ask questions
Lack of punctuality	Inability to respond to feelings of others	Inability to identify potential employers
Lack of energy	Inability to explain problems to others	Inability to identify training resources
Inability to drive a car	Inability to converse with others	Inability to identify needed community support agencies (e.g., financial and child facilities)
Inability to use public transportation	Trouble in accepting criticism	Inability to write a résumé
Inability to get up in the morning	Problems in giving directions to others	Inability to present assets to a job interviewer
Inability to perform specific physical requirements of the job	Inability to assert self constructively	Inability to answer job interview questions
	Inability to control substance abuse	Inability to perform specific intellectual requirements of the job
	Inability to get along with spouse	

Once the client's PEI problems have been identified, the list can be further organized and expanded by looking at the particular environment in which a specific deficit is a problem. The settings in which clients function can be classified as *living, learning,* and *working* (LLW). The *living* context refers to the home and community environment. The *learning* context refers to educational or training settings. The *working* context addresses places of employment. The practitioner can begin by organizing the already identified PEI problems by the environment in which they occur. Each environmental context can be explored to see whether there are further personal deficits that have not yet been identified. Also, problems that occur in one environment can be checked to see if they are also present in other environments. These additional problems will be placed in the appropriate PEI-by-LLW cell. Table 36 shows the previously identified client deficits classified PEI by LLW. Sample problems that exist in the client's environment rather than within the client have also been added. These environmental problems are classified PEI to the extent that they affect the client's ability to do something physical, to relate to self and others, and/or to perform mental activities.

As can be seen from Table 36, a single deficit may occur in more than one environmental context. This is, of course, because the client may well experience the deficit in more than one environmental setting. It is, of course, critical to consider any problems clients might experience in their living and learning environments that might have a potential impact on achievement of their career objectives (Anthony, 1979). For example, clients' inability to assert themselves in the family setting when they are overwhelmed by responsibilities and/or criticisms may eventually reduce the amount of energy and effort available for their job responsibilities. Rehabilitation practitioners will want to look for not only the more obvious work-setting problems but also any possible living and/or learning environmental problems that might impinge on the clients' attainment of their career goals.

In summary then, the practitioner will want to help clients to explore their physical, emotional-interpersonal, and intellectual problems in the living, learning, and working contexts. After ideas have been received from the client about any problems that might interfere with achievement of career goals, the practitioner can introduce potential problems based on test data, the practitioner's own professional experience, and suggestions from significant others.

The possible problems Don might have in pursuing his career goal of becoming an inhalation therapist are summarized in Table 37. The rehabilitation practitioner and Don will want to assure that the proper steps are developed and implemented so that these problems are avoided or overcome.

Table 36. Client and Environmental Deficits, Classified PEI and LLW

	Physical	Emotional-Interpersonal	Intellectual
Living	Lack of good grooming Obesity Inability to drive a car Lack of punctuality Lack of energy Inability to use public transportation Inability to get up in the morning *Lack of food, clothing, shelter at survival level	Inability to make eye contact with others Lack of temper control Inability to respond to feelings of others Inability to explain problems to others Inability to converse with others Trouble in accepting criticism Inability to assert self constructively Inability to control substance abuse Inability to get along with spouse *Refusal of spouse to be involved with treatment *Lack of available day-care facilities for children	Inability to identify support agencies Inability to budget time Inability to budget money
Learning	Lack of punctuality Lack of energy *Expense of school part-time fees *Lack of transportation to school	Inability to explain problems to others Trouble in accepting criticism Inability to assert self constructively *Poor school advisement procedures *Lack of clear directions from teachers	Inability to follow directions Inability to ask questions Inability to identify training resources Unable to perform specific intellectual requirements of the training *No assistance in securing tutor *No adult education program in community

Working	Physical	Emotional-Interpersonal	Intellectual
	Lack of good grooming	Lack of temper control	Inability to follow directions
	Obesity	Inability to make eye contact with others	Inability to ask questions
	Lack of punctuality	Inability to respond to feelings of others	Inability to identify potential employers
	Lack of energy	Inability to converse with others	Inability to write a résumé
	Inability to perform specific physical requirements of the job	Problems in giving directions to others	Inability to present assets to an interviewer
	*No public transportation near employer	Inability to assert self constructively	Inability to answer interviewer questions
	*No provision by employer of needed tools or clothes	*Reluctance of employer to rehire client	Inability to perform specific intellectual tasks required by job
		*Coworkers' unsure reactions to client	
		*Bad recommendation from past employer	

*Environmental deficit

75

Table 37.   Don's Career Problems

	Physical	Emotional-Interpersonal	Intellectual
Living		Lack of ability to control alcohol intake	
Learning			Lack of ability to present assets in an interview
Working	Lack of ability to go without smoking for long periods of time		Lack of specific intellectual skills necessary to qualify for job

Practice Situations

As a practice exercise, develop and categorize a list of problems you yourself have that might interfere with achieving your career goal. Use a format similar to Table 38. Once this exercise has been completed, you can practice exploring and categorizing career problems with a client or a friend. Remember to overview the steps involved in doing the task and to respond to the reactions you receive.

Table 38.   Sample Format for Listing Career Problems

	Physical	Emotional-Interpersonal	Intellectual
Living			
Learning			
Working			

ASSESSING PRESENT AND NEEDED BEHAVIOR

Once the problems have been identified, they need to be operationalized and assessed. *Operationalization* means to define something in observable and measurable terms. This serves to make the problem clear to both the practitioner and the client. The components required for operationalizing a client's problems are as follows:

Who?	Specifies who is performing the behavior
What skill deficit?	States the client's problem
How measured?	Specifies time (amount of time), frequency (number of times), and amount to measure the quantity of the behavior
What behavior?	Specifies the behavioral symptom of the deficit
When/where?	Specifies the conditions under which the behavior is to be performed

A format that incorporates all the above elements is: "The problem is ____[Who?]____ cannot ____[What skill deficit?]____ as measured by ____[How much?]____ of ____[What behavior?]____ is performed ____[When and where?]____." The quantification of the client's present level of functioning can be derived from client estimates, practitioner observation, role plays, simulations, or estimates from significant others.

It is important to operationalize the client's deficits for several reasons. First, operationalization will facilitate evaluating whether the client has actually overcome the deficit. Second, the mere setting of the problem in observable terms can exert a positive effect; the identification of exactly what problem(s) needs to be overcome can have a motivating effect on both the client and the practitioner. Third, it is much easier to develop a career plan if the client's problem has first been specifically identified.

The first column of Table 39 illustrates the problems that Don and the rehabilitation practitioner worked to operationalize. The operationalized definition of the problem is presented in column 2. The third column of Table 39 is the assessment column. To assess the client, the practitioner uses the operationalized problem statement as the basis from which to measure the client's functioning. As can be seen in Table 39, this leads to a specific quantitative statement about the client's level of functioning.

Once the problems have been identified and the client's present problem behavior has been assessed, the next step is to assess the client's needed level of functioning. Assessing the client's needed level (or goal) in quantified terms will ensure that both practitioner and client will be able to determine when the goal has been achieved. This builds accountability into the entire career development process. To set the goal, all that is needed is to quantify the desired level of functioning. It may be necessary to consult with people in the client's environment for help in establishing the quantified goal. This will ensure that the goals that are set are realistic.

Table 39.   Don's Operationalized Problems and Assessment of Present Level

Problem Level	Operationalized Statement	Assessment Present Level	Needed Level
Lack of ability to go without smoking	As measured by the number of cigarettes I smoke each day during working hours	20	
Lack of specific intellectual skills necessary to qualify for job	As measured by the percentage of items I could pass on the written and oral licensing test for inhalation therapist at the official examination	65	
Lack of ability to present assets in an interview	As measured by the number of job assets I have that I can identify and present in a job interview	0	
Lack of ability to control alcohol intake	As measured by the amount of alcohol I consume each day— any time, any place	20-24 oz.	

Practice Situations

Don's present and needed levels of functioning are presented in Table 40. Use these assessments as guidelines in writing your own operationalized statements. Record your statements in a format similar to Table 41. Once again, after you have completed the exercise for yourself, practice assessing career goals for a client or a friend. Be sure to respond in order to be certain that the measures accurately reflect the client's perspective. Explain the process to the client, and give examples so that she or he can actively participate. By the end of your interaction, the client should be able to accurately assess his or her own present and needed level of functioning.

Table 40. Assessment of Don's Needed Goal Level

Problem Level	Operationalized Statement	Assessment	
		Present Level	Needed Level
Lack of ability to go without smoking	As measured by the number of cigarettes I smoke each day during working hours	20	6 or less
Lack of specific intellectual skills necessary to qualify for job	As measured by the percentage of items I could pass on the written and oral licensing test for inhalation therapist at the official examination	65	72 or better
Lack of ability to present assets in an interview	As measured by the number of job assets I have that I can identify and present in a job interview	0	5 or more
Lack of ability to control alcohol intake	As measured by the amount of alcohol I consume each day— any time, any place	20-24 oz.	0

Table 41. Sample Format for Writing an Operationalized Statement and Assessing Present and Needed Levels

Problem Level	Operationalized Statement	Assessment	
		Present Level	Needed Level
1.			
2.			
3.			
4.			
5.			
6.			
7.			
8.			

DEVELOPING THE CAREER STEPS

The fourth task in getting the client to act on his or her career plans is to identify the steps that need to be taken to achieve the needed level of functioning. The needed level of functioning is the goal. The steps that are developed are the steps the client will take to reach the goal. Where the practitioner lacks the expertise to help the client reach the goal, the steps will be those the client will take to make contact with and use a resource agency. In either case, the process is the same. First, client and practitioner *brainstorm* the steps involved in reaching the goal; each step is written so that the behavior to be performed is observable. Second, they *order* the steps in terms of what comes first, second, third, and so on. Finally, they develop *substeps* to lead to the larger steps. This last part of the process is necessary only if the client does not understand how to do the steps that were initially brainstormed. Thus, the check step for an effective career route is to make sure that the client can look at the steps and say, "I know how to do each of these steps." Depending on the client, then, the career plan can range from an outline of what is to be done to a highly detailed program. Tables 42 and 43 show examples of steps developed by Don and the rehabilitation practitioner to help Don reach two of his goals.

Table 42. Don's Steps to His Goal (Example 1)

Goal: *To be able to pass licensing examination for inhalation therapist*

Step 1: Brainstorm steps

    1. Identify where to get training
    2. Complete courses
    3. Apply for training position
    4. Decide where to go
    5. Take licensing exam

Step 2: Order steps

    1. Identify where to get training
    2. Decide where to go
    3. Apply for training position
    4. Complete courses
    5. Take licensing exam

Step 3: Develop substeps (as needed)

    1. Identify where to get training

        a. Call hospital and get official name and number of licensing board

        b. Call licensing board and ask for approved training programs

    2. Decide where to go

        a. Develop values

        b. Research and do decision-making steps

    3. Apply for training position

        a. Call alternative programs for application procedures

    4. Complete courses

    5. Take licensing exam

        a. Ask people in program about whom to see on how to prepare

        b. Follow preparation instructions

Table 43. Don's Steps to His Goal (Example 2)

Goal: *To be able to identify 5 assets that would convince the program admissions people to accept me and to be able to present the assets in an interview*

Step 1: Brainstorm steps

1. List at least 5 assets
2. Practice answering interview questions with assets
3. List past school and work experiences
4. Identify "dependability" assets
5. Identify "getting along" assets
6. Identify "ability to do job" assets

Step 2: Order steps

1. List past school and work experiences
2. Identify "dependability" assets
3. Identify "getting along" assets
4. Identify "ability to do job" assets
5. List at least 5 assets
6. Practice answering interview questions with assets

Step 3: Develop substeps (as needed)

1. List past school and work experiences

2. Identify "dependability" assets

    a. Look at overall attendance
    b. Look at attendance in science courses
    c. Look at punctuality at school and work
    d. Look at on-time completion of assignments

3. Identify "getting along" assets

    a. Look at arguments with teachers or supervisors
    b. Look at arguments with peers
    c. Look at elected offices in school
    d. Look at friendships

4. Identify "ability to get a job" assets

    a. Look at overall GPA
    b. Look at GPA in science-related courses
    c. Look at GPA in laboratory
    d. Look at honors received (formal or informal - e.g., compliments on work)
    e. Look for interview behaviors that show ability to function under pressure
    f. Look at work experiences that show ability to function under pressure

5. List at least 5 assets

    a. Pick from above 5 assets that would impress an interviewer most

6. Practice answering interview questions with assets

    a. Check with people now in program to find out how questions are asked
    b. Practice using assets to answer these questions

83

Practice Situations

Now you should develop steps to reach each of your goals. Use a format similar to Table 44 as a way to record your plan steps. Upon completion of this practice exercise, work with a client or a friend to practice developing steps to his or her operationalized goal. It will be critical for the client's future independence that he or she be able to modify and/or develop steps to reach goals. To the greatest extent possible, try to help the client understand the process. In working with the client on this exercise, overview the three steps involved in developing a plan, do one example with the client, and then let the client take the lead in creating the steps. Your role as practitioner will be to respond to the steps that are developed by the client, to initiate missing steps, to ensure that the steps are written as behaviorally as possible, and to check to be sure that the client knows how to do each step in the program.

Table 44.   Sample Format for Developing a Career Plan

Goal: _____

Step 1:   Brainstorm steps

   _____

   _____

   _____

   _____

   _____

Step 2:   Order steps

   1. _____

   2. _____

   3. _____

   4. _____

   5. _____

Step 3:   Develop substeps (as needed)

   1. _____

      a. _____

      b. _____

      c. _____

   2. _____

      a. _____

      b. _____

      c. _____

ACTING TO DEVELOP A CAREER PLAN: A SUMMARY

Goal: To identify the steps in the career plan.

1. Identify and categorize problems that may interfere with attainment of the career goal.

> Ask the client to identify the problems that might inhibit attainment of the career goal.

> Explore the client's physical, emotional-interpersonal, and intellectual deficits.

> Look at the particular environment (i.e., living, learning, or working) in which a specific deficit is a problem.

> Introduce problems based on test data, professional experience, or suggestions from significant others.

2. Assess present and needed level of behavior.

> Define the problems in observable and measurable terms.

> Define the present and needed level of functioning in quantified terms.

3. Develop the career steps.

> Brainstorm with the client the steps involved in reaching the goal.

> Order the steps (i.e., first, second, third).

> Develop substeps that lead to the larger steps (if necessary).

ACTING TO IMPLEMENT CAREER PLANS

SPECIFYING NEEDED RESOURCES

Once the steps in the career plan have been identified, they must be implemented. In developing the steps in his or her career plan, the client may well have explicitly indicated the need for the use of community resources — resource people, or agencies. However, the resources may not have been specified. If this is the case, the practitioner will want to work with the client to specify the resources that will be used. When the resources are specified, the chances are increased that the career plan will actually be implemented.

Specification of people resources can include *what* agency, *where* it is located, *who* the contact person is, and *how* the contact will be made. If it is not possible to get a name, the position of the person to be contacted can be identified. Specification of things resources can address *what* resource, *where* it is located, and *how* to obtain it.

Thus, if one of the client's goals were to get a job in a specific occupation, one step might be to identify employers with job openings. The client would then identify the specific resource to help accomplish this. In this case, the specific resource goal could be identified as follows:

What?:	State Employment Service
Where?	2401 Main Street
Who?	Ms. Harriet Jones
How?	Personal visit

Identifying a contact person may require an initial call. The extra effort is worthwhile because many clients feel more comfortable when they have a person to contact rather than an agency.

In his initial development of steps, Don indicated that he would be using several resources. These are specified in Table 45. A resource can be used for either a step or a substep.

Table 45. Specific Resources Needed to Complete the Steps in Don's "Licensing" Plan

Goal: *To be able to pass licensing examination for inhalation therapist*

Steps		*Resource*	
1a.	Call hospital and get official name and number of licensing board	*What?* *Where?* *Who?* *How?*	City Hospital 1359 Chestnut Street Personnel Department By phone
3a.	Call alternative programs for application procedures	*What?* *Where?* *Who?* *How?*	Hospitals that have program To be obtained from list Personnel Department By phone
5a.	Ask people in program about whom to see on how to prepare	*What?* *Where?* *Who?* *How?*	People I know in program Not applicable Teachers, students Face-to-face talk

Practice Situations

Specify the resources that you would need to complete the steps in your career plan, using Table 46 as a format for recording your information. Then, work with a client or a friend to specify the resources necessary for her or his career-route implementation. Be sure to be explicit about the what/where/who/how strategy so that the client can later duplicate the process.

Table 46. Sample Format for Specifying Resources

Goal: _____

    _____

Steps   *Resource*

___   _____   _____

       _____   _____

       _____   _____

___   _____   _____

       _____   _____

       _____   _____

___   _____   _____

       _____   _____

       _____   _____

ASSIGNING COMPLETION DATES

The final step in the career development process is to assign completion dates to each of the major steps in the program. These timelines will serve to give both the practitioner and the client a clear indication of whether or not progress is really being made. In other words, it is an additional way to ensure accountability. With the dates assigned, the issues of what will be accomplished and when it will be accomplished are both addressed. In order to develop time lines, the practitioner will want to help the client explore and understand realistic completion dates. One mechanism for doing this is to estimate the number of hours required to complete the task and then to estimate the average number of hours per week the client can spend working on the task.

For example, Don estimated that he could spend about five hours a week working to identify his assets and present them to an employer. Since he and the practitioner estimated that the process would take about ten hours, Don initially decided that the final step could be completed in about two weeks — approximately one step every two days.

If other people are to be involved in helping the client reach the goal, their schedules, of course, will also need to be considered. For example, Don shortly realized that he could not do a good job on step 4, his performance assets, without getting his school transcript. He realized this would take about three weeks. Therefore, he rearranged his time schedule. The time line he developed for his program is presented in Table 47.

Table 47. Time Line for the Steps of Don's "Assets" Plan

Goal: *To be able to identify 5 assets that would convince the program admissions people to accept me and to able to present the assets in an interview*

Steps	Completion Dates
1. List past school and work experiences	2/7
2. Identify "dependability" assets	2/9
3. Identify "getting along" assets	2/11
4. Identify "ability to do job" assets	2/25
5. List at least 5 assets	2/27
6. Practice answering interview questions with assets	3/1

In addition to time lines, it may also be necessary to develop differential reinforcements to accompany each goal or major step. That is, if in the practitioner's judgment the client needs some external consequences to ensure step completion, then a positive and a negative reinforcer can be assigned to that step or combination of steps. Since identifying assets was the most difficult part of Don's program (steps 2, 3, and 4), he and the rehabilitation practitioner decided that some extra incentives would be appropriate. They decided that when he had completed all three steps he would buy himself a new shirt. (Don was the kind of person to whom clothes were important, and this reward would be motivating for him.) If Don did not complete the steps within the specified time, he would have to give his favorite shirt to one of the charity organizations that recycled clothes.

Practice Situations

Now you can develop time lines for each of the major steps in your own career plan, using a format similar to Table 48. Then work with a client or a friend, and repeat the process. Be sure to explain the thinking behind the development of the time lines and reinforcements so that the client can fully participate. After taking the initiative in developing the first couple of dates, check the client out by having him or her develop the rest of the time lines. You can then explore the client's thinking behind the times suggested. Also, for practice, write at least one complete plan, and record it using a format similar to Table 48.

Table 48. Sample Format for the Career Plan

Goal: _____

Completion
Dates

Steps

Step 1: _____ _____

    a. _____ _____

    b. _____ _____

    c. _____ _____

Step 2: _____ _____

    a. _____ _____

    b. _____ _____

    c. _____ _____

Step 3: _____ _____

    a. _____ _____

    b. _____ _____

    c. _____ _____

Step 4: _____ _____

    a. _____ _____

    b. _____ _____

    c. _____ _____

Step 5: _____ _____

    a. _____ _____

    b. _____ _____

    c. _____ _____

Possible reinforcements: _____

_____

ACTING TO IMPLEMENT THE CAREER PLAN: A SUMMARY

Goal: To help the client complete the steps of the career plan and reach the career goal.

1. Specify the resources needed to complete the steps in the career plan.

2. Assign completion dates to each of the major steps in the career plan.

   Explore with the client realistic completion dates.

   If necessary, develop differential reinforcements for each step.

ACTING ON THE CAREER CHOICE: A SKILLED APPROACH

Sara wasn't taking any chances that Jim might blow it. She really wanted to see him make it in the career area he had chosen. And she knew quite well that, in order for this to happen, they would have to prepare things very carefully.

"The first thing we've got to do is pinpoint any trouble spots there might be," she told Jim. By "trouble spots," she meant particular physical, emotional, or intellectual problems that might come between Jim and his chosen career as a computer programmer.

In fact, exploration did serve to reveal several areas of potential difficulty. Of these, the most important seemed to be Jim's tendency to fly off the handle when subjected to even a minimal amount of pressure from other people.

"OK, then," Sara said, "this is obviously a 'working' as well as a 'living' problem. And even though the job you want will involve only minimal interaction with other people, you're certainly going to have to work with some people some of the time. For that matter, you're going to have to deal with people just to get the job! So what we really need to do is define your problem in this area in concrete terms and then develop a sort of program to solve it."

In the end, they decided that Jim could best deal with this particular problem by developing some specific interpersonal skills designed to give him an understanding of another person from that person's own frame of reference. Sara herself could train Jim in the new skills he would need — listening, observing, responding, and so on.

Once they had worked on a specific way to deal with each of Jim's problems, Sara worked with him to develop an effective program of action to get where he wanted to go. The computer programming course at the local college was available only to full-time students registered in other programs. But the local technical school offered an excellent program at night that would take Jim only one year to complete. Meanwhile, he could obtain a part-time job to see him through.

They dealt with these and a host of other considerations. In the end, Jim had developed a sequential, step-by-step program that spelled out nine major tasks he would have to complete in order to secure a position as a programmer. Each of these major tasks or steps entailed several substeps. And at every step, Jim would be able to evaluate his progress to date and make sure that he was on track and functioning within the time frames he and Sara had established.

Before Jim left the office that day, Sara was careful to schedule another meeting with him in a week's time. She knew that it would be important to him to be able to check back with her on a regular basis.

"I've learned a whole lot from this," Jim told her, hesitating in the doorway. "I always knew that you could deal with — oh, you know — dumb machines and stuff in a systematic kind of way. But I always thought people just had to act the way they felt like acting. It's really good to know that it doesn't have to be like that."

Sara nodded. "It feels good to know that you can approach your own life in a careful, logical manner, instead of just letting things happen."

"Uh-huh." Jim nodded his agreement. "And the funny thing is, I feel more like a real person that I did before. I mean, having people do stuff in a really organized way might sound like the people were just turning into machines. But it's just the opposite. Now I know that I can really get to wherever I want to go. I'm not stuck anymore. I can be me!"

Chapter 5 EVALUATING THE EFFECTIVENESS OF CAREER COUNSELING

Evaluation of the effectiveness of the career counseling process can be conducted at both *outcome* and *process* levels. The basic outcome measure for career counseling is whether or not the client enters and remains in an occupation with which she or he is satisfied. A refinement of the technique of self-report satisfaction involves using the values and favorability scales that were developed with the client earlier to evaluate the position the client obtains. The average favorability score obtained by the job can then be used to determine just how favorable that particular position really is.

At the process level, career counseling success can be evaluated in terms of the career-development knowledge of the client. The more the client knows about how to approach the career development process, the greater are the chances for success. The basic assumption of this type of evaluation is that client effectiveness can be used as an evaluation measure of the practitioner's effectiveness. An evaluation checklist for career development is presented in Table 49. The checklist indicates the criteria that determine whether the client has reached an effective performance level in the area of career development. As can be seen from the checklist, there are both summary and individual criteria. Summary criteria indicate whether or not the client can perform the behavior that is the end product of each of the three career development phases. The individual criteria examine the client's capacity to perform each of the component behaviors in each of the three career development plans. If the client can meet the summary criteria, then the individual criteria need not be evaluated.

In addition to its use in evaluating the effectiveness of the career counseling process, the checklist may also be used as a diagnostic instrument. That is, it can be used prior to the beginning of the career counseling intervention to assess the client's relative strengths and weaknesses in the career development area. A comprehensive diagnosis will tell the practitioner the particular areas on which the counseling process must focus.

This comprehensive diagnosis is also helpful to the practitioner who refers clients to various agencies and facilities that specialize in specific aspects of the career counseling process. By using the checklist, the practitioner can make a much more detailed and comprehensive referral. As a result, the practitioner will be able to spell out specifically what she or he expects the agency to accomplish and, in so doing, will be much more capable of evaluating whether the agency has been able to bring about the desired client career outcomes.

Using the checklist prior to career counseling also gives the practitioner a perspective on his or her effectiveness. This is because data on both the client's prefunctioning and postfunctioning will be available. The checklist represents the performance criteria. The practitioner needs to develop questions around each of these items in order to elicit the information from the client necessary for evaluation. The questions that are developed can be administered either orally or in written form. The evaluation method used will depend on the client's reading and writing skills. In general, unless the client is functioning at an achievement level of at least seventh grade in reading, an oral test should be administered. If possible, it is preferable to have the client answer the questions in writing, as this is an easier form to score and will save the practitioner time.

The assessment, whether written, oral, pre-, or post-, does not need to take place in one sitting. It can be done by major phases (i.e., exploration, understanding, action), by skill groups, or by individual skills. The questions can also be reworded to fit a particular client population.

It is particularly important that the practitioner use the evaluation instrument, at least in the postcounseling process, during the early stages of his or her use of career counseling skills. This is the most effective method for obtaining short-term feedback on one's efforts.

Table 49. Evaluation Checklist for Career Development

		Yes	No
I. Exploration measures			
A. Summary criterion			
1. The client is able to list at least three occupational alternatives congruent with her or his interests and educational level.		____	____
B. Individual criteria			
1. The client can identify at least six values that are important to him or her in choosing a job.		____	____
2. The client is able to articulate some of her or his abilities and deficits in relation to the world of work.		____	____
3. The client is able to articulate a specific area of interest in which to explore possible occupations congruent with her or his values.		____	____
4. The client is able to articulate a specific educational level, congruent with her or his abilities, in which to explore occupational alternatives.		____	____
II. Understanding measures			
A. Summary criterion			
1. The client is able to use all of her or his values and to consider the relative importance of these values in identifying a realistic and satisfying job goal.		____	____

Table 49 — *Continued*

	Yes	No

B. Individual criteria

1. The client is able to identify exactly what each career value means to her or him. ____ ____

2. The client is able to indicate what would be acceptable and unacceptable levels of satisfaction for each of his or her career values. ____ ____

3. The client is able to differentiate the relative importance of her or his values. ____ ____

4. The client is able to indicate at least ten types of resources that could be used for getting information about jobs. ____ ____

5. The client possesses the following information about at least three jobs in his area of interest and level of education. ____ ____

   a. education and training requirements ____ ____

   b. personal qualifications ____ ____

   c. major tasks performed ____ ____

   d. proportion or amount of time spent on each task ____ ____

   e. salary ____ ____

   f. opportunities for advancement ____ ____

   g. types of employers ____ ____

   h. working conditions ____ ____

   i. supply and demand ____ ____

6. The client can demonstrate a career decision-making method that evaluates potential job alternatives on the basis of their capacity to satisfy each of the client's career values. ____ ____

III. Action measures

A. Summary criterion

1. The client can articulate a step-by-step plan of action to achieve his or her career goal. ____ ____

B. Individual criteria

1. The client can articulate observable problems that could interfere with her or his career plans. ____ ____

2. The client can articulate observable goals that he or she must reach in order to attain his or her career objective. ____ ____

3. The client can develop at least five steps to reach her or his operationalized goals in such a way that she or he knows how to do each step. ____ ____

4. The client can set realistic time lines for implementing his or her career programs. ____ ____

5. The client can articulate positive and negative reinforcements for completing the steps of the career program. ____ ____

REFERENCES

Anthony, W. A. *Principles of psychiatric rehabilitation.* Amherst, MA: Human Resource Development Press, 1979.

Bozarth, J. D., and Rubin, S. E. Empirical observations of rehabilitation counselor performance and outcome: Some implications. *Rehabilitation Counseling Bulletin,* 1975, September, 294–298.

Cannon, J. R., and Pierce, R. M. Order effects in the experimental manipulation of therapeutic conditions. *Journal of Clinical Psychology,* 1968, *24,* 242–244.

Collingwood, R. R. The relationship between career objectives and recidivism. Manuscript, City of Dallas, 1976.

Friel, T.W., and Carkhuff, R.R. *The art of developing a career helper's guide.* Amherst, MA: Human Resource Development Press, 1974.

Holland, J. *Making vocational choices. A theory of careers.* Englewood Cliffs, NJ: Prentice-Hall, 1973.

Hoppock, R. *Occupational information.* New York: McGraw-Hill, 1976.

Isaacson, L. E. *Career information in counseling and teaching.* Boston, MA: Allyn & Bacon, 1977.

Pierce, R. M. *Master plan for adult corrections.* Frankfort, KY: Kentucky Department of Justice, 1975.

Pruitt, W. *Vocational evaluation.* Menomonie, WI: Walter Pruitt Associates, 1977.

Super, D.E. *The psychology of careers: An introduction to vocational development.* New York: Harper Row, 1957.

Truax, C. B., and Carkhuff, R. R. *Toward effective counseling and psychotherapy.* Chicago, IL: Aldine, 1967.

United States. Bureau of Labor Statistics. *Occupational outlook handbook.* Washington, D.C.: Government Printing Office, 1978.

United States. Employment Service. *Dictionary of occupational titles.* Washington, D.C.: Government Printing Office, 1977.